STYLISH WEDDINGS for LESS

STYLISH WEDDINGS for LESS

HOW TO PLAN YOUR DREAM WEDDING ON A BUDGET

BY CATHERINE SABINO

filipacchi
publishing

First published in 2009 in the
United States of America by
Filipacchi Publishing
1633 Broadway
New York, NY 10019

Design: Patricia Fabricant
Editor: Lauren Kuczala
Production: Lynn Scaglione
and Annie Andres

Prices, addresses, telephone numbers
and websites listed in this book are
accurate at the time of publication but
they are subject to frequent change.
Source material and recommendations
are not intended to be comprehensive,
but rather representative.

ISBN-13: 978-1-933231-65-5

Library of Congress Control Number:
2009923653

Printed in China

CONTENTS

INTRODUCTION

Welcome to *Stylish Weddings for Less*. Even before the recent economic downturn, couples looked for smart ways to maximize their wedding dollars. And for good reason—with the average cost of a wedding at $21,814 last year (dropping from $28,704, according to The Wedding Report), that's still a hefty price tag for an event that lasts just a few hours.

Excitement, tension, frayed nerves and unintended melodrama frequently come into play when planning any big event, and if that big event is a wedding, well, expect double helpings of all of the above. So it's easy to see how the bottom line, or wedding budget, gets lost in the whirl of emotions—sense yielding to sensibility, with guest lists growing, and sudden sticker shock when presented with the final tab.

We hope *Stylish Weddings for Less* will help you avoid unnecessary wedding-cost stress and budgets gone amok. As many planners and brides will tell you, once the word "wedding" is used as an adjective (as in wedding reception, wedding dress, wedding cake), prices soar! In each chapter of this book there are dozens of ideas on how to get the most for your wedding expenditures. We help you find the best pricing for everything from bridal dresses to reception sites; suggest the most cost-effective ways to buy flowers, rings and invitations; and get the inside scoop from top wedding and honeymoon planners, caterers, lighting specialists and photographers on working within a budget. For the DIY-er, we have ideas for making bouquets, invitations and reception decorations.

There are plenty of cost-saving ideas online, of course. The millennial wedding experience is a most interactive one, with brides reaching out to one another for information and blogging about their planning experiences in extraordinary detail. And it only takes a few seconds of Googling to see the wedding category is an extremely vast one—there's almost too much information to digest, as many a bleary-eyed, Web-surfing about-to-be-married couple can attest. With so many sources, which to check out? In addition to our experts' and real couples' advice, we point you in the direction of many of the most useful wedding sites to save you time, money—and eyestrain!

If there's one thing you should take away from this book, it's that you don't have to go into debt to have a stylish wedding. Even celebrities are practicing the fine art of scaling back for their march down the aisle.

We extend our best wishes for your upcoming nuptials. May your wedding day be everything you hoped it would be: chic, fun, memorable—and affordable!

CATHERINE SABINO

CHAPTER 1

LOW-KEY CELEBRITY WEDDINGS

Say "celebrity wedding" and the words "huge bash" come rather quickly to mind. And for good reason: Who can forget reports of Tom Cruise and Katie Holmes's three-day destination wedding in Rome that ended with a ceremony and reception in a castle, and a tab of about $3.5 million?

When Nicole Kidman married Keith Urban near Sydney, there were many boldfaced names among the 230 guests, with no less than the Wolverine himself, Hugh Jackman, providing the reception entertainment. Catherine Zeta-Jones wed Michael Douglas in a million-dollar extravaganza at New York City's Plaza Hotel that forced even jaded Manhattanites to take note. When you're living a red-carpet life, how can your wedding be anything but over-the-top?

But in these cautionary and eco-conscious times, the bling patrol is on alert. And too much may well be too much. Amy Sultan, editor of *CelebrityBrideGuide.com*, points out that more and more celebs are opting for low-key, and often less pricey, nuptials, for a number of reasons. "The desire for privacy is huge, so guest lists are cut way down; the press—even family and friends—are often told after the fact. With the economy being what it is, many don't want to look insensitive with a showy event. And celebrity brides are into green and eco-conscious weddings. So this also plays into the more subdued vibe that's popular now."

Marcy Blum, an event planner in New York City who has coordinated weddings and events for a number of boldfaced names, adds, "Celebrities are choosing to spend their money in ways that don't make outrageous statements. They keep their weddings small, but then pick up the hotel and airfare for all the guests. It's a quieter way to be lavish."

Sultan says the lower-key celebrity wedding now takes on one of four forms.

✳ **The surprise wedding** "Guests think they're just going to a party. And then—surprise!—the couple ends up getting married. That's what Julia Roberts did."

✳ **The courthouse wedding** "With just the bride and groom and witnesses in attendance." (See Jessica Alba, and others, page 11.)

✳ **The green wedding** Kaitlin Olson and Rob McElhenney of *It's Always Sunny in Philadelphia* had a nature-themed wedding at Saddlerock Ranch in Malibu. The bride told *InStyle* she wanted their wedding "to produce as little waste as possible."

✳ **The restaurant wedding** Keri Russell married Shane Deary in New York City on Valentine's Day in 2007, followed by a small reception at The Harrison restaurant in Tribeca.

20 SMALL CELEBRITY WEDDINGS OF NOTE

THEY MARRIED AT HOME

✳ **Julianne Moore** wed her longtime beau, director **Bart Freundlich**, in a simple ceremony in the backyard of their Greenwich Village, New York, townhouse, where a reception for 36 was also held.

✳ Singer **Mary J. Blige** married record producer **Kendu Isaacs** at her home in Bergen County, New Jersey. Her mother and sister prepared the reception food for 50 guests.

✳ **Mariah Carey** wed singer and actor **Nick Cannon** at her house in Eleuthera with a small gathering of family and friends.

✳ The 50 guests at **Julia Roberts'** wedding to cameraman **Daniel Moder** thought they were going to a Fourth of July party at her Taos, New Mexico, ranch. At least that's what the invitations said. The wedding reception was a barbecue.

✳ *Vogue* editor-in-chief **Anna Wintour** wed child psychiatrist **David Shaffer** in 1984 at their Greenwich Village townhouse, where the wedding dinner for 20 guests was also held.

✳ **Demi Moore** and **Ashton Kutcher** were married at their Beverly Hills home. There were 45 guests.

✳ **Dennis Quaid** wed **Kimberly Buffington** at his Montana ranch with nine guests in attendance.

✳ **Woody Harrelson** married former assistant **Laura Louie** at home in Kipahulu, Maui, with a handful of friends (Sean Penn, Alanis Morissette) sharing in the celebration.

✳ **Steven Soderbergh** wed entertainment reporter **Jules Asner** at Soderbergh's Manhattan apartment with a few family members and friends looking on.

NO GUESTS, PLEASE!

✻ **Jennifer Garner** married **Ben Affleck** in a super-private ceremony (the only people in attendance were the actor Victor Garber, who was the officiant, and a witness) at the Parrot Cay Resort in the Turks and Caicos.

✻ **Jessica Alba** wed **Cash Warren** at the Beverly Hills Courthouse. There were no guests.

✻ **Gwyneth Paltrow** married **Chris Martin**, also without guests (not even Blythe Danner!), at the San Ysidro Ranch in Santa Barbara.

✻ **Tori Spelling** tied the knot with **Dean McDermott** on a private island in Fiji. There were no guests.

✻ **David Letterman** married longtime girlfriend **Regina Lasko** at the Teton County Courthouse in Choteau, Montana. Son Harry tagged along.

✻ **Matt Damon** wed **Luciana Bozan Barroso** at New York's City Hall. Luciana's then 7-year-old daughter was in attendance.

✻ **Ellen Pompeo** married record producer **Chris Ivery** at New York's City Hall with NYC Mayor Michael Bloomberg and deputy Mayor Patricia Harris as witnesses.

KEEPING IT SMALL

✻ **Maggie Gyllenhaal** and **Peter Sarsgaard** married at the Convento di Santa Maria di Costantinopoli, in Brindisi, Italy. There were 40 guests.

✻ **Carla Bruni** wed the president of France, **Nicolas Sarkozy**, in a civil ceremony in the Élysée Palace. Only 30 guests were invited.

✻ **JFK, Jr.,** married fashion publicist **Carolyn Bessette** in Cumberland Island, Georgia. The ceremony was held in the First African Baptist Church. A reception for 40 followed at the Greyfield Inn.

✻ **Scarlett Johansson** married **Ryan Reynolds** at the eco-friendly Clayoquot Wilderness Retreat in Tofino, British Columbia. Thirty to forty guests came along for a destination-wedding weekend, where they were told to enjoy the great outdoors as much as they could during their stay.

CHAPTER 2

"REAL" BRIDES: WHAT they SPENT and HOW they SPENT IT

We spoke to five couples around the country with budgets ranging from $10,000 to $25,000 about how they produced their memorably stylish weddings. Their receptions ranged from brunches to sit-down dinners, the guest lists from 60 to 150, the brides' gowns including vintage finds as well as a rented designer dress.

Prioritizing was the key to maximizing their wedding dollars: For one couple an innovative reception menu was important; for another an extensive photography shoot. Creative talents came to the fore, with many couples designing their own invitations, programs, flower arrangements and decor.

Late fall brunch in Austin

COUPLE: Alyson Fox, an artist, and Derek Dollahite, owner of Coloring Book Studio, an interactive design agency

DATE: Sunday, November 2, 2008

BUDGET: $10,000

GUESTS: 108

PHOTOGRAPHER: Ashley Garmon

✳ **Venue/reception:** The brunch was held at Mercury Hall, an event space and chapel dating from the early 20th century. For a Sunday in November, the venue fee was **$1,500**, which included 100 folding chairs. Two extra-large tables and white tablecloths were an additional **$120**.

The brunch, which consisted of four kinds of breakfast tacos, vegetable casseroles, pumpkin muffins, brownies, cookies, chocolate truffles, and fresh fruit, cost **$3,200**; the liquor, **$700**, included two different kinds of Champagne and beer.

✳ **Cake:** A family friend, Alice Ward, made the marzipan cake with Swiss dot-style icing. It was her gift to the couple.

* **Flowers:** "My mother-in-law, Terri Dollahite, bought an assortment of flowers including hydrangeas, cosmos and eucalyptus leaves, and white pumpkins at the Austin Flower Company, a local wholesaler. The flowers, in our white-black/plum color scheme, cost about **$700**. The hand-potted succulents served as take-home favors in addition to our "tie-the-knot" kits (see opposite) and were an extra **$130**.

  "We spent about **$90** for containers in various sizes. Terri and her friends arranged the flowers—I wanted a casual, straight-from-the-garden feel for the bouquets and centerpieces. We also created origami flowers for the ceremony and reception decor."

* **Music:** **$250** for a pianist at the ceremony; an iPod playlist for music during the brunch.

* **Gown:** "I designed it myself with the help of a seamstress, who created a muslin pattern. The fabrics were from a parachute dating from World War II and a vintage kimono. Underneath the dress I wore a vintage slip from the 1890s. The total cost was **$800**."

* **Groom:** A Band of Outsiders suit, purchased wholesale and not part of the wedding budget.

* **Bridesmaids and groomsmen:** They paid for their own clothes. "My sister, the maid of honor, purchased her dress on eBay for **$14**."

* **Ring:** Fox bought a white-gold band ring for her husband for **$225** online. "My ring was vintage, and did not come from the budget."

* **Invitations:** Fox designed the invitations and had them printed at Sesame Letterpress in Brooklyn. Total cost: **$180**. Recycled envelopes: **$25**. Postage (60 invitations were sent): **$25**, with an RSVP to the couple's website.

* **Photography:** **$1,500** for still photographs from Ashley Garmon Photographers. "We had a 'friends and family' discount," says Fox. "The fee ordinarily would have been $3,000. There was no videography."

* **Favors:** Emergency sewing kits (a play on "tying the knot") with imagery from the invitation, **$120**. Other gifts: Vintage lockets for Fox's sister, two flower girls and the pianist as thank-you mementos. Two vintage pins for her mother and mother-in-law. Total cost: **$195**.

* **Website:** "We already had an interactive site, so we didn't need to create a new one."

'20s–'30s-style dinner reception in Boston

❋ Venue/reception: "I researched extensively," says Miller. "As government-owned properties have the most reasonable fees, we decided on the Commandant's House, a lovely mansion overlooking Boston Harbor. We wanted a Saturday evening wedding, so by having it in January we saved a lot (fee: **$2,000**). The ceremony was at 5 p.m. and the reception followed.

"Instead of going to a caterer, I networked through friends and found a chef who would prepare a menu for us. He obtained the insurance he needed to work at the Commandant's House on our wedding day and hired his own assistants. We gave him a budget and asked him to be as creative as he could be within it.

"For appetizers, we had tuna tartare, arancini, and beef-skewer hors d'oeuvres. There was a buffet for the entrée course with gourmet pizzas (one with duck, another a goat cheese and shrimp combination, and a vegetarian pizza), pasta salads and green salads.

"We wanted an open bar, but limited the drink service to wine (a Chardonnay and Merlot) and beer. Our wines averaged **$10** per bottle. For the toast, we served Prosecco, also about **$10** a bottle. We bought the liquor ourselves from a store with a buy-back policy. Our total catering costs, with liquor, were **$2,900**.

"For the reception decor, I rented gold tablecloths and ivory napkins and tied them with satin ribbons. I bought dozens of ostrich feathers online for about **$150** for the centerpieces. To make the tables look extra-special (we had six tables seating 10), I rented a higher-end china. My husband, who is a graphic artist, designed Art Deco–style mini–paper lanterns with electric tea lights, which we placed on tables and at key spots—on mantelpieces and along stairways—throughout the house.

"As the ceremony was at the same site, we just had to add a few more touches. We found an aisle runner at Ikea (actually panel curtains we sewed together) and sprinkled it with rose petals (total cost under **$100**). My sister made small bouquets for the aisle decor. She bought embossed gold paper,

COUPLE: Virginia Miller, freelance writer, and Patrick Barry, graphic artist for Houghton Mifflin

DATE: Saturday, January 10, 2009

BUDGET: $15,000 (final cost: $13,500)

GUESTS: 60

PHOTOGRAPHER: Robert C. Mirani

created cone-shaped flower holders (seaming together the sides with hot glue) and filled them with mini-carnations. They were each tied to a chair at the end of each aisle with beaded string." Total decorating costs: **$2,200**.

✻ **Cake:** "We didn't have one. We served three mini-desserts instead—a banana crème pie, green tea cakes, and mini-cupcakes." Total cost: **$335**.

✻ **Flowers:** "My sister bought pink roses at a local wholesaler and made my bouquet. She mixed in white feathers to tie in with the centerpieces and wrapped the bouquet with hot-pink ribbon. We also made the boutonnières— a pink rosebud and a small feather wrapped with gold wire, with an oversize gold pin to attach to the lapel." Cost: **$150**.

✻ **Music:** "While searching for a display gramophone on Craigslist, we actually stumbled across a gramophone collector and expert, Bruce, who agreed to come to the wedding and play music from the '30s and '40s during our cocktail hour. The cost was about **$200** and it couldn't have worked out better. For the reception, I created the playlist and hired another DJ. Because it was off-season, I was able to negotiate a great fee." Total cost: **$800**.

✻ **Gown and groom's attire:** A 1930s-style bias-cut dress, very old Hollywood glamour in feel, purchased through a wholesaler, Vows, in the Boston area. "Instead of a veil, I used a feather headpiece. Since it was winter, I wore a fur stole—it was vintage. My husband found his tux at a vintage shop, Bobby from Boston. All we had to do was change the buttons. His shirt was from Brooks Brothers." Cost of dress and accessories: **$1,800**. Groom's clothes: **$345**.

✻ **Bridesmaids:** "My bridesmaids didn't carry flowers, so that was a cost saving. Also, I didn't want them to go through the expense of a new dress, so I asked that they wear something either in gold or silver that would be suitable for a black-tie event."

✻ **Invitations:** "Since our wedding had a '20s–'30s theme, Patrick made invitations displaying the shape of a gramophone—the placecards also had this shape. He cut and lettered each invitation, as well as the seating cards." Cost: **$200**.

✻ **Photography:** Still photography from Robert C. Mirani: **$1,000**. "Friends took turns with a video camera—and the results were great!"

* **Favors:** "We made them ourselves, placing chocolates in satin pouches, then tying them to a balloon with a placecard. After guests found their spots, they either attached the balloons to their chairs or let them free to float to the ceiling, lending another nice decorative touch."

* **Miscellaneous:** Ceremony officiant, **$200**; gifts for groomsmen, **$150**; for bridesmaids, **$150**; catering insurance, **$1,000**.

* **Advice for DIY-ers:** "You need to set aside the time and have a great support team. Doing the decorations took all our free time for two weeks. Marrying off-season helped, we were able to go to the venue the day before to set up. We wouldn't have been able to access the event space ahead of time during a busy period."

A ceremony and cake reception in Atlanta with an edge

COUPLE: Ashley Summerlin, graphic designer, and Dusty Meaders, a systems analyst

DATE: Saturday, October 20, 2007

BUDGET: $15,000

GUESTS: 150

PHOTOGRAPHER: Our Labor of Love

✱ **Venue/reception:** Studio Ninehundred in downtown Atlanta for both the ceremony and reception. "This cost **$900** for the entire day, but we had access to the studio the day before to prepare," says Summerlin. "The decoration costs were minimal. I bought Chinese paper lanterns in bulk for a total of **$45**. We decorated them with cupcake liners (**$6**), which were glued to the lanterns (another **$6**). For the ceremony, we made flower holders from containers purchased at Ikea (**$16**), covering them with fabric. We added red carnations to each and tied one to every other aisle of chairs. Rental for chairs was **$620**.

"For the reception, we borrowed two tables from home to hold the cake and the candy bar. We covered the tables in red fabric (**$80**), and bought vases at Ikea (**$100**) that the florist filled with red dahlias. We spent about **$65** for napkins, plates and forks. Little fabric birds, which topped our wedding cake,

were also used in the wedding invitation box, on tables, and even in the bouquets. I made them myself (fabric costs: **$80**). The cake stand was made by stacking several cardboard cake boards and then covering them in red fabric (**$20**). We found a birdcage in my parents' basement, spray-painted it white, and used it as decoration and for anyone wanting to drop off a gift or card at the reception (no cost)." Total cost: **$1,938**.

✽ **Cake:** "We just had cake and ice cream at the reception. The four-tier cake with vanilla filling and white cream icing was **$675** from Matty Cakes bakery in Atlanta. Ice cream was **$660** with Ben & Jerry's sending someone to serve. We organized the candy bar so that we had red and blue candy (**$150**) to pick up our color scheme. There was no hard

liquor, just soft drinks (**$250**). We bought galvanized steel buckets at Home Depot (**$20**), and filled them with Izzes and sodas in vintage-style bottles. Total cost: **$1,755**.

✽ **Flowers:** "We worked with a local florist, Little Sparrow Floral Design, and asked for an interesting mix of red flowers. We had dahlias,

carnations, celosia, viburnum berry, and a few red vanda orchids for special touches. Cost for all bouquets and flower decorations, **$1,360**."

✳ **Music:** iPod playlist for ceremony and reception.

✳ **Gown:** "It definitely was one of the big-ticket items, a Suzanne Ermann gown, purchased at Kelly's Closet in Atlanta for **$3,250**. The Chie Mihara shoes I bought on eBay for **$68**."

✳ **Bridesmaids and groomsmen:** The couple's gift to their bridal party was their wedding attire. Two Betsey Johnson bridesmaid dresses cost **$600**, two pairs of bridesmaid shoes from Anthropologie, **$70**. The groom's and groomsmen's suits were purchased at Zara, **$700**; Ralph Lauren shirts, **$150**; shoes (Converse) and socks, **$120**.

✳ **Invitations/programs:** "As a graphic designer, I was able to do the letterpress invitations and the wedding programs myself. The invitations were placed in a small box, with a decorative bird." Favors consisted of candy in a glassine bag, letterpressed with a "Thank you for coming to our wedding" note. (Total cost of the paper goods and wedding boxes: **$700**, plus **$125** for postage.)

✳ **Photography:** "For **$4,620**, our package included an engagement shoot, seven hours of photo coverage on our wedding day (there were two photographers), as well as a smile booth, where photos of each guest were taken. We worked with Our Labor of Love, a studio in Atlanta."

✳ **Website:** Already established.

Botanical garden wedding
in Southern California

COUPLE: Christa Scott, freelance writer, and Travis Goldstein, stockbroker

DATE: Saturday, November 15, 2008

BUDGET: $25,000 (final cost: $23,000)

GUESTS: 95

WEDDING PLANNER: Beth Helmstetter

PHOTOGRAPHER: Meg Perotti

✳ **Venue/reception:** Hartley Botanica, Somis, California. "We loved the beauty of these gardens," says Scott. "I would recommend choosing a site that has the look you want without needing to change much. We didn't have to decorate, which saved a lot of money. Since we married off-season, we had a really good rental rate, **$2,000**.

"We opted for a buffet, so guests could mingle easily. Our extended families had yet to spend time together, so this was a good way for them to do it. We brought in our own caterers—as we married off-season and in a down economy they were able to work within our budget.

"I'm from South Carolina, and since it wasn't practical for us to be married there, I insisted on having a Southern menu: Southern fried chicken, mashed potatoes served three ways in martini glasses with different toppings. For appetizers, we limited them to three hors d'oeuvres—five would have been a lot more expensive. We had a cheese station as well.

"There was no question we would have anything but a full bar. It's what makes a good party. We bought our own liquor at Costco, so the total cost was only **$300**. Before the ceremony, we served hot cider, sweet tea and lemonade. For the toast, we went with a mid-price Champagne." Catering costs: **$9,000**.

✳ **Cake:** "We had three different cakes—each a single layer and with a simple fondant frosting. One was red velvet (if you're from the South, you have to have that!), the others were chocolate-raspberry and cinnamon spice. We added flowers around the cake display rather than have elaborate cake decorations, which saved money. The cakes ran about **$500**."

✳ **Flowers/decor:** "The centerpieces were a mix of white hydrangeas and candles. We bought glass hurricanes in bulk for the candles. The florist had candles

"real" brides: what they spent and how they spent it

that had been burned once, so we were able to get many of them for half price. We wanted a mostly candlelit event, but we hung a few lights from the trees. There were little touches, too. We tucked dried rather than fresh lavender (less expensive) into each napkin." Flower costs (personal and for reception): **$1,000**.

✳ **Music:** "We had a DJ and made up a request list, and asked him to fill in the rest." Fee: **$2,000**.

✳ **Gown:** "I had to have a Vera Wang and rented one from One Night Affair. It ended up costing **$1,500**—not sure that was a huge savings."

✳ **Wedding party:** "No bridesmaids. Just flower girls, so that saved on some costs."

✳ **Wedding planner:** "I definitely recommend having one. They can offer a lot of creative ideas and save you time and hassles. We worked with Beth Helmstetter of Beth Helmstetter Events." Fee: **$2,700**.

✳ **Invitations, programs, menus, placecards:** $500.

✳ **Photography:** Still photography by Meg Perotti. Cost: **$2,500**. "No wedding album—we're taking the files to Kinko's. My husband will do any retouching. As for videography, a film editor friend from Disney wanted to build a video portfolio, so he shot our wedding for **$800**."

✳ **Favors:** "We wanted to keep them Southern-themed. We bought mason jars in bulk at Costco and my mother filled them with peach pie filling." Cost: **$500**.

Destination wedding in Florida

COUPLE: Kristin LaMarre, sales executive, and Trent Snyder, teacher

DATE: Saturday, October 25, 2008

BUDGET: $25,000

GUESTS: 81

WEDDING PLANNER: Leana Gallagher

PHOTOGRAPHER: Thomas Hager

✱ **Venue/reception:** Late-afternoon ceremony and evening reception at The Ribault Club, a Southern-style mansion on Fort George Island, Florida. Why a destination wedding? "We had our budget," says LaMarre. "If we stayed in Philadelphia, we could see our guest list growing to 200 or so. We preferred to have fewer guests and the type of wedding where we could enjoy being with friends and family over a long weekend rather than for four hours. The venue fee was **$3,850** and our travel and hotel costs were **$3,500**, but that included our being in Florida for 10 days.

"We held the ceremony under an oak tree at dusk. We were in a beautiful spot so there was no need for extra decoration—just simple white chairs. We had a drink station before the ceremony, serving citrus-infused water and Pimm's Cups.

"For the reception we also kept it simple. We used white tablecloths, accented by brown napkins wrapped in pink ribbon, picking up the color of the flowers and bridesmaids' dresses. For each table, we had three small vases filled with a mix of dark pink carnations and roses. Vintage-style baseball cards were used to indicate seating arrangements. Simple white Christmas lights and lanterns were strung between trees over the dance floor. For all the reception decorations, we spent about **$400**.

"We're foodies, so we wanted an untraditional menu. We supplemented the hors d'oeuvres with an artisanal cheese station. For the entrée course, we had braised ribs, local grouper, stuffed cabbage leaves, shrimp and grits. We didn't want a cake, so we had a dessert station, serving petit fours and mini-cheesecakes.

"The wine was purchased locally, with both reds and whites about **$9** a bottle. But we kept an open bar. I'm not sure you save that much by only having wine and beer—people just end up drinking a lot of wine and beer. We went with an inexpensive Champagne for the toast. Our liquor cost was **$900** (for wine, liquor for a full bar, Champagne, and beer), and overall catering costs, **$5,586**."

✳ **Flowers:** "For personal flowers, we used roses, ranunculus and stock. Bridesmaids had smaller versions of the bouquet I carried. We spent **$915** for personal and reception flowers."

✳ **Music:** A DJ was hired for **$800**.

* **Gown:** "I loved a Monique Lhuillier gown, but it ran about $7,000. There's a very good dressmaker, Kate Ramos, in Philadelphia. I asked her to make something similar and the dress ended up costing a lot less, **$2,100.** The flowers for my hair were **$50,** shoes, **$125.**"

* **Wedding planner:** Leana Gallagher, Amelia Occasions, **$2,500.**

* **Invitations and Save-the-Dates:** $1,000.

* **Photography:** "We had stills and videography. It was easy to negotiate rates off-season; Thomas Hager Photography's fee for the print photos was **$2,650.** We have the disc for the stills and will create a wedding book ourselves. The videographer was a friend of a friend. He was building his film portfolio and did a wonderful job, charging only **$700.**"

* **Favors:** Baseball cards and biscuits (included in overall reception costs).

* **Guest book:** "Instead of a traditional guest book, we bought various postcards from the island and had guests write us a note. After we left, our wedding planner mailed them to us. They trickled in over a few days and we adored reading all the words of love and well-wishes."

CHAPTER 3

GOWNS and WEDDING ATTIRE

The holy grail of bridal dresses—a Vera Wang or a Monique Lhuillier—can set you back $7,000 or more, a noticeable chunk out of any but the most lavish wedding budgets (although Vera Wang, nodding to the demands of the recession, recently lowered the median price of her gowns from $5,500 to $3,800).

But there are plenty of options for the bride who doesn't want an expensive gown—everything from vintage to buying from one of the e-discounters offering those Vera or Monique dresses at a fraction of the cost.

HOW TO MEASURE

"When ordering a gown online, your measurements should be slightly under those of the dresses you're considering," says Julie Jones, owner of *EncoreBridal.com*.

Have your measurements taken by a professional if possible. Measure with the underpinnings you plan to wear on your wedding day.

BUST: At the largest part.

WAIST: Generally an inch above the belly button. Do not pull measuring tape tight, like a belt.

HIPS: At the widest.

DRESS LENGTH: From shoulder seam, straight over the bust, to waist, down to floor (or desired hem length).

SKIRT LENGTH: From waist to floor (or desired hem length). Wear the heel height you plan for your wedding shoes.

When buying a dress

✳ **Plan on spending 4–6 weeks** to find a gown, more if you're looking to save big bucks.

✳ **Ideally, have the dress chosen six months** before your wedding date.

✳ **The general rule is to set aside 6%** of a wedding budget for your gown, but you can get away with far less. When figuring the cost, factor in alterations, dry cleaning (if a sample or pre-worn), underpinnings, veils and accessories.

✳ **Best deals at bridal shops** and department stores are often between Thanksgiving and New Year's.

✳ **Look beyond the bridal department.** As you pay a premium for anything labeled "bridal," shop for long gowns in white or ivory (or whatever color you want) in other sections of your favorite department stores.

✳ **Bridal sizing will typically run two to three sizes higher** than what you'd normally wear. So don't panic if you're normally a size 6 (termed "street size" in wedding speak) and the gown that fits is a size 10. Size charts vary from manufacturer to manufacturer, so have your measurements taken professionally (see left) before ordering online.

✳ **Planning on a photo session** prior to your wedding day? Factor in that date for having your gown ready.

* **Where you're getting married and the time of year** should determine the gown's fabric, e.g., if you're having a beach wedding, skip the heavy beading, silks and satins, and opt for cotton, cotton/sateen or lace. Sounds obvious, but sometimes easy to overlook if you fall in love with a particular design.

* **For fittings or try-ons,** wear the undergarments closest to what you'll wear on your wedding day. This applies whether you're having a gown custom made or picking one off the rack at a sample sale.

* **During wedding gown alterations,** make sure to take along shoes with the same heel height as those you'll wear on your wedding day.

* **Your dress should have a label** stating the manufacturer/distributor/retailer/fabric content, where it was made and care instructions—whether you're buying full retail or at a discount outlet. It's an FTC regulation for vendors to provide this information. Print out a copy of the FTC's "Wedding Gown Labels: Unveiling the Requirements" at *ftc.gov*. Certain bridal shops have been known to cut out labels to prevent bargain-hunting customers from researching dresses on their time, and then purchasing them through a discounter. While a store can remove a manufacturer's label and replace it with its own, showing or trying to sell a gown that doesn't have the FTC-mandated information is illegal.

Vintage

There are a lot of good reasons to go vintage for your wedding gown—aside from the stylish recycling and cost savings, you'll get the superior workmanship and exquisite fabrics associated with dressmaking from long ago, as well as dress cuts and silhouettes not available from bridal designers today. "Vintage" is a broad term, applying to about a 60-year period (1890s–1950s), although some shops and websites carry pieces before or after those dates. So that means you'll find everything from '20s flapper styles and '30s Harlow-inspired satin columns to '50s-era tulle fantasies à la Grace Kelly. In addition to vintage and consignment shops and vintage dress fairs, look into what the auction houses nearest you might be offering (be sure you can give the dress a try-on before bidding). If you've never bought from a vintage dealer before, check them out at *vintagefashionguild.org*. If you decide to go vintage, here's what to keep in mind:

SIZING AND ALTERATIONS

✳ **Most vintage pieces** correspond to today's sizes 0–6 (50 years ago and earlier, women tended to have smaller builds).

✳ **Even with smaller builds,** other-era brides used some mighty serious underpinnings, like a corset, to slip sleekly into their gowns. So when considering vintage, buy something that fits comfortably with the undergarments you want to wear, or be sure the dress can be let out. Remember, the goal is a fabulous dress with "wearing ease." Don't buy a tricky-to-alter vintage piece based on plans to lose a certain amount of weight by the time your wedding rolls around.

BEING SMART ABOUT VINTAGE

Cherishedbride.com's Jennifer Hollon specializes in vintage bridal wear. Here's her advice on shopping and caring for vintage:

• **AVOID DRY-CLEANING IF YOU CAN.** Too many old fabrics dissolve with the chemicals used by cleaners today. A competent handwashing is sometimes all you need. Keep in mind that many vintage dresses were made from rayon satin. Rayon is a washable fiber, so gowns often just need a good shampoo soak in the tub. (Remove buttons, as they can rust; zippers weren't used in many older garments.)

• **OLDER LACES CAN BE BRITTLE AND DRY,** so they may require more care in handling and wearing. Expect slight tearing.

• **THE GOWNS THAT SELL MOST QUICKLY** are from the '30s and '50s—big, poufy dresses that Sarah Jessica Parker has made popular—and '60s A-line styles. If you're going to buy vintage, learn about the various decades' styles, so you can focus on the silhouette you want and find the right accessories.

Opposite: When searching for vintage, '50s-era pieces turn up on many brides' short list. At Posh Vintage (*poshvintage.com*), three recent offerings included, from left, an ivory strapless wedding gown with a tulle skirt; a light coral antique lace and pearl tea-length dress; and a pink organza tea-length, all dating from the 1950s.

✳ **How much can you alter vintage?** That's the big question. It's always easier to take in than go up a size, but in the hands of the right tailor or seamstress, some additional enlargement might be possible. Many older pieces have wide seam allowances, but let-out fabric might not match outer fabric, which could have faded somewhat over the years.

✳ **Older gowns** can sometimes be lengthened with contrasting fabric or vintage lace panels, and those with full skirts taken in for a less billowy silhouette.

✳ **The condition of the fabric** will determine how extensive and what kind of alterations your dressmaker will be able to make. Do a "stress test"—a good idea even if the dress fits you perfectly. Check key seams at the shoulders, underarms, waist and along the zipper. Many vintage shops work with certain tailors and seamstresses, so before you buy, consult with one they recommend and be certain of what they can do with the dress.

✳ **Factor in alternation costs,** generally from $75 to $250, when deciding whether to go vintage. You may also want to budget for lace restoration fees and button replacement. And set aside time to allow for several fittings.

✳ **As with any alteration,** make sure it's done in a clean work space. No need to add 21st-century stains to your 1920s dress.

VINTAGE WEDDING DRESS STYLES

1900s: Edwardian-style high-lace necklines, leg-of-mutton sleeves, fitted bodices and slim skirts

1920s: Flapper-style, with beading and trim

1930s: Jean Harlow–inspired sleek satin columns; bias-cut lace and satin gowns

1940s: WWII-era satin gowns, with padded shoulders and sweetheart necklines; trim waist and slim skirts, often with trains

1950s: Wide ball-gown skirts; full-skirt tea-length dresses

1960s: A-line satin silhouettes à la Jackie Kennedy

ALTERING VINTAGE

Diane Ackerman, owner of The Threadbender (*thethreadbender.com*), which specializes in the restoration and alteration of vintage and contemporary gowns:

"When it comes to alterations, I feel anything is possible. I took a size 4 dress and made it a size 22!"

- MANY VINTAGE GOWNS have long trains, so that's where you get the extra fabric. The tightest fit with most vintage pieces is in the bodice, but as long as there's extra fabric, we can recreate it.

- WE USE THE SEWING TECHNIQUES of the period—so how you alter a '20s dress differs from one from the '30s.

- YOU CAN GET RID OF most fabric's yellowing, but rust stains are tough. We sometimes use beadwork to cover stains.

- IDEALLY, A BRIDE SHOULD ALLOW up to six months for extensive alterations. Most alterations start at $200, the average running between $400 and $600.

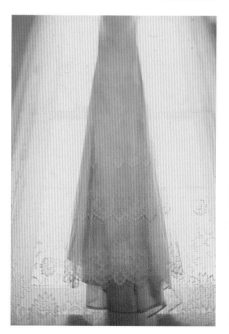

STAINS

It can be hard to remove a stain from yesterday's dinner party, never mind one that's reached vintage status itself. While some stains are removable, you should check with a cleaner first.

✳ **Before you buy,** scrutinize the dress in broad daylight for stains, discoloration or yellowing spots.

✳ **The average local dry cleaner** may not be able to do the job, and if you are asked to sign a release absolving it from any claims should something happen in the cleaning process, don't go there! A good cleaner should be able to tell you what they can and can't do and back up their work.

✳ **Find cleaners with a track record** with vintage; better, one with a specialty in cleaning bridal vintage, or seek out an archival cleaner. If you don't have one in your area, go to *heritagegown.com*, which specializes in cleaning and preservation.

✳ **Consider the cost:** A cleaner specializing in vintage can charge up to $200 to get your dress in pristine shape; higher fees are not uncommon. Ask for an estimate first and try to get it in writing.

New "old"

✳ **If you can't find the vintage piece you want,** but still would like a period look or cut, consider buying a vintage pattern and having the dress made for you (see page 57). For wedding dress patterns from other periods, go to *sovintagepatterns.com* and *voguepatterns.com*.

✳ **A number of online sites** offer reproductions of period gowns; it may not be the real deal, but at least you'll find your size and you won't have to worry about the fabric condition.

❧ SOURCES: *Online Vintage*

While it might seem risky to buy vintage online, the good sites have detailed and realistic descriptions of a gown's condition and return policies. Never buy without a fair return option.

ANTIQUEDRESS.COM (go to the Wedding section) Pieces from the early 20th century to the 1990s. Even the recently spotted white jersey gown once owned by Whitney Houston might work as a wedding piece. From $395.

CHERISHEDBRIDE.COM Specializing in dresses from the '30s to '60s, from as low as $149, with many gowns in the mid $600 range. Lovely accessories collection.

POSHGIRLVINTAGE.COM From the '40s to '70s, generally priced from around $325.

VINTAGEVIXEN.COM Good selection of '50s and '60s gowns and "new old" from other periods. Detailed gown descriptions. From $125.

VINTAGEWEDDING.COM Reproduction Victorian and Edwardian. Good selection of 1940s pieces. From $175.

Pre-owned contemporary

Wear a gown that was recently worn by another bride on her wedding day? Not everyone is comfortable with that idea, even if they're OK with vintage (while all vintage is pre-owned, not all pre-owned, obviously, is vintage). "We have customers ask about the karma of a wedding dress before they decide to buy—did the couple stay together—but we don't get into that," says Laura Fluhr, owner of Michael's, a well-known New York consignment shop. But if the gown's recent past is of little concern to you, buying a pre-owned can save big bucks, landing you a coveted designer dress at a fraction of the cost. You'll also have a wider selection of gowns to choose from than you would with vintage. Shop consignment stores and online; some websites specializing in pre-worn gowns are so detailed that you can even search by designer, style and size. Keep in mind:

✽ **Condition:** Should be spotless. When buying pre-owned contemporary, you shouldn't have to foot the bill for dry cleaning. If the dress is a few seasons old, you won't have to worry about fabric fading, but check for stains and tears, particularly with beading and fine lace.

✽ **Original cost:** Many shops ask to see the gown's purchase price before accepting for consignment. When you've zeroed in on a dress, you may want to see it as well.

✽ **Alterations:** You'll have more latitude than with vintage, but remember the two-sizes-down, one-size-up rule (you can take a dress down two sizes or enlarge it one dress size), but again, it depends on the style and fabric.

✽ **Re-consigning:** If the dress you wore is in top shape and a desirable style, you may be able to re-consign to the shop you bought it from. "It all depends on how great the dress is and its condition," says Laura Fluhr of Michael's.

✽ **E-shopping:** "Make sure the site or seller has a fair inspect-and-return policy before ordering," says Julie Jones of *EncoreBridal.com.*

WEDDING GOWNS ON EBAY

You can get a tremendous deal on eBay, but you can get stuck with a lemon, too. EBay has countless wedding gowns for sale, many imported from the Far East. But caveat emptor! Even though the pictures advertising the gowns may be from prestige bridal designers and manufacturers, the gowns may be knock-offs. To get a good deal from this site:

✽ **Look for close-outs** from manufacturers or stores going out of business, or end-of-season (late summer; between Thanksgiving and Christmas) bridal salon clear-outs.

E-BOUTIQUES

BRAVOBRIDE.COM Everything from $100 Oleg Cassinis to Vera Wangs for under $1,000 (although you can easily go higher). Discounted Monique Lhuillier, although well into five figures.

ENCOREBRIDAL.COM Gowns from $1,000 to $3,000, averaging 30%–70% off designer names like Elie Saab, Badgley Mischka, and Christos. Generous 7-day return policy. All consigned pieces must have retailed for at least $2,000. Showroom: 3215 Highland Ave., Manhattan Beach, CA 90266; 310-545-1409.

ONCEWED.COM Includes used, new and sample designer wedding dresses ranging from $100 to $5,000. Over 2,000 designer gowns in their database, with many selling for more than 50% off the retail price. Vera Wang, Monique Lhuillier, Melissa Sweet and Reem Acra are some of the labels.

PREOWNEDWEDDINGDRESSES. COM A wide range of price points and designers, from J. Crew to Oscar de la Renta.

SAVETHEDRESS.COM Conveniently organized by price and best value. A recent perusal showed a new Givenchy gown for only $550 and a Vera Wang at 13% its original cost. Many never-worn and new-with-tags items.

WOREITONCE.COM Good selection of under-$500 gowns; wide range of sizes.

➻ SOURCES:
Consignment Shops

ATLANTA: Bridal Sense, 6600 Roswell Rd., Atlanta, GA 30328; 404-256-4696. Pre-worn and new, from $99.

CHICAGO: I Do Designer Bridal Consignment, 6742 West Belmont Ave., Chicago, IL 60634; 773-205-1234. Pre-owned as well as vintage. From $300.

DALLAS: Anonymously Yours, 9310 Forest Lane, Suite 204, Dallas, TX 75243; 214-341-4618. This shop mixes pre-owned (about 30% of stock) with sample and discontinued wedding gowns, from $99.

NEW YORK: Michael's Bridal Salon, 1041 Madison Ave., New York, NY 10075; 212-737-7273. Where New York socialites unload (and, *shhhh!,* sometimes buy) their gowns. Vera Wang, Badgley Mischka, Carolina Herrera are typical labels. From $395 to $2,500 for gowns originally $2,800–$12,000.

WASHINGTON, DC: I Do I Do Wedding Gowns, Gaither Center, 15932 Luanne Drive, Gaithersburg, MD 20877; 240-243-0050. Over 1,400 pre-owned and designer close-out gowns, from $150 to $5,000.

* **Buy from a Power Seller,** or if you can't, check buyer feedback. Get the seller's home and work phone numbers.

* **A gown for sale** can never have too many pictures! Make sure the posting has plenty of them before you buy, and that you can return the item.

* **Go with PayPal,** never write a check or wire cash.

Rentals

Rent your wedding gown? A trend that's gained in popularity in recent years, particularly in California, thanks to celebrities renting and borrowing gowns for their big red-carpet moments. (And consider, men have been renting their wedding attire for years.)

✳ **Best for:** Those not big on nostalgia, who don't see their gown as a treasured keepsake. There's no guarantee your daughter or other family member will want your dress when she ties the knot years from now. Besides, two to three decades is a long time to be dealing with a big box taking up space in your closet.

✳ **Figure out what you're really saving.** Generally expect to spend between $200 and $600 for a good rental. Could you buy something from a discounter for the same price? Check to see if the rental package includes dry cleaning and accessories, like a veil or headpiece, shoes and underpinnings.

✳ **Realize only minimum alterations** are permitted when renting.

✳ **Reserve the moment you find what you want.** A gown can often be placed on hold for up to 5 months, even if you haven't set your date.

✳ **Renting is a great option for bridesmaids** and flower girls. If you can't get your bridesmaids to agree on a dress they might want to own, go the rental route (bridesmaids pay for their rentals).

❧ SOURCES: *Dress Rentals*

Renting isn't big online yet. Many rental stores have websites to give an idea of what's in stock, but most require an in-person visit.

ALEXANDRIASFORMAL.COM Over 2,000 rental gowns. Complete rental packages from $230, plus costs of cleaning. A wide range of sizes. Store: 112 Main St., Roseville (Sacramento), CA 95678; 916-787-0900.

LLRENTAL.COM Has licensed dealers throughout the country. Also bridesmaid and flower girl dresses.

ONENIGHTAFFAIR.COM Gowns used for TV and movie shoots, worn an average of 1–3 times. Runway samples, manufacturer close-out styles as well. Over 1,500 gowns from $100 to $1,000 in sizes 4–30. Store: 1726 S. Sepulveda Blvd., Los Angeles, CA 90025; 310-474-7808.

Sample sales

After the wholesale bridal market held each year in New York, bridal shops and departments stores are eager to unload dresses that haven't sold to make way for new stock. Sample sales can range from relatively low-key affairs that go on for several weeks to frenzied one-day "blowouts," as they are often described. While sample sales can take place whenever a retailer or manufacturer wants to get rid of stock, November–February are big months, with July–August not far behind. When shopping sample sales, keep in mind:

✴ **There are strict no-return policies.**

✴ **Condition:** While no bride may have waltzed down the aisle in these dresses, they can show signs of wear and tear, so inspect carefully, regardless of how good a deal a dress may seem.

✴ **A sample sale can be a combat zone.** Come early, bring a friend who can help you scoop up dresses to try on, wear a leotard so you can strip down, even amid the racks, if need be, to try on a gown. Veterans of the Vera Wang and Filene's sales suggest having friends wear brightly colored clothing (to spot in a crowd), with cell phones (to locate them) at the ready, and leave the handbag at home.

✴ **You might get a good deal pre–sample sale.** Since most bridal shops have some form of sample sale, find out when it is, you may strike a deal for the gown you've been eyeing before it hits the racks.

❧ SOURCES: *Sample Sales*

DAVID'S BRIDAL (*davidsbridal.com*) Ongoing discounts and sample sales, online only. No-return policy for sample items. In store, many low-cost gowns.

DEMETRIOS February. 222 West 37th St., New York, NY; 212-967-5222. From $249, sizes 4–26.

FILENE'S RUNNING OF THE BRIDES Held at certain Filene's stores throughout the country once a year and twice a year at the Boston headquarters, these events attract so many customers and generate such frenzy and bedlam that TV stations and newspapers rarely fail to cover them. Major bridal labels from $249 to $699. Racks can be stripped bare in less than a minute. Fresh stock throughout the day, for those who miss the opening bell. Check *filenesbasement.com* for dates.

HITCHEDSALON.COM Online site for the Georgetown, D.C., shop has a sample sale section. Sample gowns (usually "wedding size" 10, "street size" 6 or 8) are up to 70% off, but you need to call for prices. 202-333-6162.

KLEINFELD "Blowout" sales four times a year; by-appointment sample sales monthly. Iconic New York City bridal store carries all the big names. Dresses from $499. 110 West 20th St.; 646-633-4300.

MONIQUE LHUILLIER Sample sales held in July and November, usually at a pop-up store in downtown Los Angeles. Gowns 40%–90% off. Call main store for info: 323-655-1088.

SAKS FIFTH AVENUE holds Bridal Sample Sales from January to May. Top designers are up to 50% off. Open a Saks account the day you purchase and get an additional 10% off. To find the time of the sale nearest you, go to the "Stores and Events" link at *saksfifthavenue.com*.

VERA WANG December. People travel from all over the country for this sale, with lines forming hours before the doors open. While Vera Wang is located at 991 Madison Ave., NYC, the sales are usually held at the New Yorker Hotel, 481 8th Ave., 9 a.m. to 5 p.m. Date of sale usually posted on *verawangonweddings. com* in November, or check with the corporate office, 212-575-6400.

Bridal discounters

There are a number of retail outlets and what seems to be a constantly growing number of websites devoted to discounted in-season (or one or two seasons old) gowns. The discounts aren't limited to a day or a couple of weeks as they are with sample sales. In the bricks-and-mortar version, what you see is what you get. If you're buying from an online-only discounter and are not familiar with its reputation, there are a number of precautions you should take:

✳ **Research the site:** Go to *ripoffreport.com* and look for Wedding Services; *weddingwire.com*; or *consumeraffairs.com/weddings*. The Better Business Bureau is also a good source, but you'll need to know the state in which the site is registered. Another way to check is to join a wedding forum and ask about the vendor you want to buy from.

✳ **Check the return policy.** Make sure it has one you're comfortable with to get a gown back on time for full credit, usually minus a restocking fee, shipping and insurance costs.

✳ **Know what you're buying.** Does the site/store promise discounted designers or copies?

✳ **Give yourself a time cushion in case of shipping errors.** The best sites have good track records, but there's always the risk of human error, which means you might end up with a dress in the wrong size or color; dubious sites might send a copy or a worn dress—or even no dress at all!

✳ **Use a credit card for a deposit.** It will give you more leverage in case you're unhappy with the service.

❧ SOURCES: *Bridal Gown Discounters*

ONLINE

BRIDALONLINESTORE.COM A distribution center over 25 years old, which recently added a store in Covington, KY, and Maui. 195 different house styles with discounts of up to 80% off comparable retail gowns. Three-day return unless custom. 866-694-6967.

BRIDECOUTURE.COM While there's a store in San Diego, if you can't make it there, you can purchase up to four gowns without a restocking fee. Most gowns, from name manufacturers, are samples from retail stores. 50%–75% off, sometimes starting as low as $399. Seven-day return policy. Store: Bride Couture, 13443 Standish Drive, Poway, CA 92064; 858-842-2220.

BRIDEPOWER.COM Higher-end gowns, 50%–75% off, but most cost $999 and up. Three-day notification for returns, plus shipping and insurance costs. Store: Vows Bridal Outlet, 334 Watertown St. (Rt. 16), Newton, MA 02458; 866-THE-GOWN.

EBRIDALSUPERSTORE.COM Many top manufacturers represented at up to 40% off. Sizes 0–50. From $138. Recommends underpinnings and shoes for each gown. All sales final. 4–16 weeks for delivery.

GOWNBIDDER.COM Ongoing auction for gowns from about a dozen manufacturers. Most are overstock and samples.

NETBRIDE.COM A discounter in business since 1948. Guarantees originals from name manufacturers, 30%–50% off. Items not returnable unless gown is shipped in wrong size, color or style.

PERFECTBRIDAL.COM Find your dream gown and send them the manufacturer/designer and style number, and they'll provide a price quote by phone. A Brides of California company, which has been in business since 1965. As all items are made to order, there are no returns.

RKBRIDAL.COM The no-frills website for the no-frills store in New York City, with many discounted high-end brands. They say they'll better the lowest price of any gown from an authorized online dealer by 5%. Store: RK Bridal, 318 West 39th St., New York, NY 10018.

SHOPFORBRIDAL.COM Mostly accessories, some bridesmaid dresses, and dresses for beach weddings.

STORES/SHOWROOMS

GLAMOUR CLOSET carries bridal samples and overstock from boutiques and department stores around the country, with such names as Vera Wang, Monique Lhuillier, Carolina Herrera, Reem Acra and many others. All off the rack, so you can browse without an appointment. Prices generally 25%–75% off. Annual sample sale (usually in December) for even bigger savings. Locations: 114 Columbus Ave., San Francisco, CA 94133; 415-391-1515; and 324 S. La Brea Ave., Los Angeles, CA 90036; 323-938-2000.

NEIMAN MARCUS LAST CALL, with stores throughout country, usually in outlet malls, often carries bridal gowns up to 80% off.

SHOWROOMS: The Bridal Building, 1385 Broadway, New York, NY 10018; 212-764-5769. Twenty-four stories of bridal manufacturers that sell mostly to the trade, but are open to the public 9–3 on Saturdays, by appointment only. Up to 30% off retail. Credit card policies vary among manufacturers.

The custom option:
Have your gown made
(or make it yourself)

You want a little of this dress and a bit of that, but it hasn't come together in one fabulous gown and you're tired of looking. Why not have your dream dress made for you? Here's how to do it:

✱ **Find a dressmaker experienced with bridal wear.** Get referrals from your tailor, fabric store, even bridal shops, which may work with one for alterations. If the dressmaker hasn't done bridal, then choose someone skilled with making cocktail dresses and gowns and who has worked with special fabrics.

✱ **See samples of their work.** If there is time, have something made for you before committing to the gown.

✱ **When designing a gown with your dressmaker,** first, get an idea of the basic silhouette you want. Collect tear sheets; go to *weddings.ivillage.com* and click on Build Your Dream Wedding Dress—it's an easy and fun way to start the process.

✱ **Ask if they create a muslin sample;** it's the best way to go.

✱ **Insist on three to four fittings**—before and after the lining is sewn in; prior to hemming; and a final fit for the bodice.

✱ **Consider the final cost.** Having a dress made may not be the least expensive dress option. Factor in the dressmaker fees, fabric, linings, trims, special laces and beadwork, etc. Get an estimate from your dressmaker—in writing—before proceeding.

✱ **Dare to sew it yourself?** You can find bridal gown patterns at *voguepatterns.com, simplicity.com, mccallpattern.com, sovintagepatterns.com.*

✱ **If you're buying fabric online** (e.g., *housefabric.com, bridalfabric.com*), ask for a sample first. Remember, cut fabric isn't returnable.

Right: For many "green" weddings, recycled chic is the way to go, with vintage fabric, embroidered trim, and embellishments coming together in stylish new ways.

ONE GOWN OR TWO?

When you're cost-conscious, having a wedding dress for the church ceremony and another for the reception—a growing trend in recent years (think high-profile brides like Katie Holmes and Christina Aguilera)—might be beyond your budget. Yet, if you still want something that's formal enough for a church or synagogue but won't hamper your style when you want to rock out on the dance floor during the reception:

- **LOOK FOR GOWNS WITH** detachable trains or two-piece dresses—switch out a fuller, more elaborate skirt for a sleeker, reception-ready version.

- **IF YOU DO BUY A SECOND GOWN,** try to select a style that doesn't require a change of lingerie, shoes, hairstyle or jewelry.

Non-bridal retailers

Retailers like J. Crew, Banana Republic and Ann Taylor can be great resources for reasonably priced bridal gowns or bridesmaid dresses—the type they're likely to want to wear again.

✳ **J. Crew:** An ever-growing popular collection of clean-lined gowns, from $295. Bridesmaid dresses from $165 and a flower girl selection, too. A wedding specialist will help coordinate your wedding party's purchases. Liberal return policy. *jcrew.com*

✳ **Ann Taylor:** Check out the "Weddings and Events" collections for bridesmaids. Wide range of sizes, 00–18. Free return on "Weddings and Events" items. *anntaylor.com*

✳ **Other sources for bridesmaids:** *Bananarepublic.com:* a small selection of cocktail-length and long dresses, from $175 to $275; *spiegel.com* for cocktail dresses.

Headpieces and veils

Many of the discount bridal sites listed earlier in this chapter sell veils at reasonable prices. In addition, there are numerous websites specializing in veils and offering good value: *visionveils.com, weddingveil.com, illusionsbridal.com, everafterbridalveils.com, veilshop.com.*

✳ **Making a veil is also a simple project for a tailor.** Buy tulle in the tone closest to your gown and the length you want. Then select a headband or comb attachments and whatever embellishment you like—often these items are available at fabric stores. To make a veil yourself, go to *save-on-crafts.com* and type in "veil."

✳ **Don't want to go the veil route?** Have your hairstylist arrange a series of beautiful brooches in your hair.

Bridesmaids

Many sources in this chapter have gowns/dresses for bridesmaids. Brides today offer their bridesmaids flexibility in what to wear, focusing on a color, leaving bridesmaids to then decide on the style dress they want.

And now about the groom...

If you're carefully watching your wedding budget, you're probably not going with a formal daytime or evening wedding. "Casual stylish" or "casual elegant" is how many couples classify their weddings today, and that allows for creativity and more options for the groom and his attendants' wear.

But for protocol sticklers, here are the tried-and-true guidelines:

Very formal/formal daytime: A cutaway (morning coat), waistcoat, striped trousers

Very formal evening: Black tailcoat or tails

Formal evening: Tuxedo, or black dinner jacket and matching pants

Semiformal day: Stroller-cut jacket and pants in dark color

Semiformal evening: Black dinner jacket and matching pants

Informal day or evening: Sharp business attire

Rent a tuxedo or buy? Depends on whether the groom thinks he'll wear one more than a few times in the next several years. *Buy4LessTuxedo.com* carries Calvin Klein, Ralph Lauren, Joseph Abboud, Armani and other labels at discounted prices. J. Crew (*jcrew.com*) is another option for a tuxedo, with a jacket recently priced for $450, pants $195.

Tuxedos generally rent from $50 to $200 (approximately 10% to 30% of retail), the higher end for the modern, most stylish options (which is what he'll want). If the groom and his groomsmen are going with tuxes, get everything at the same store (if geography permits); there are usually discounts with multiple rentals. (Often the groom's tux is thrown in for free with four or more rentals.) Men's Wearhouse (*menswearhouse.com*) has locations throughout the country for tux rental and purchase.

Or just skip the protocol (there are no wedding fashion police, after all) and have the groom wear the best suit he owns. Add an ivory tie to make it wedding-ready. Ask all the groomsmen to wear either a navy, charcoal gray, or black suit that they already own. On a recent scroll through *OnceWed.com*'s "Real Weddings" section, grooms at a number of very stylish weddings were wearing business suits, particularly pinstripes with brightly colored ties (to match the bridal party colors).

For summer/warm climate/destination weddings, the khaki or chino suit is a great option. Navy blazers and chinos are also popular, or for that Gatsby look, navy blazers and white flannels.

gowns and wedding attire

CHAPTER 4

The WELL-PRICED RING

For years, grooms-to-be have been told to budget about two months' (pretax) salary for a ring. But the recent taste for bigger rocks has made that guideline obsolete, considering that the average groom is 27 or 28 when he marries and just starting out on a career. The average cost of an engagement ring runs between $3,000 and $6,350, depending on the survey and the part of the country you're in. At Tiffany & Co., a one-carat ring in their best known setting starts at $8,500.

Engagement rings

As with any consumer purchase, the more you know about what you're buying, the more informed decision you can make. And a little knowledge goes a long way when purchasing gems and rings, particularly when you're trying to save money. The Gemological Institute of America (*gia.edu*) has a good primer on what to look for when you're buying a diamond. But basically it gets down to knowing about the four *C*'s :

✳ **Carat weight** Gems are measured in carats, with each carat weighing about ⅕ of a gram. Carat weights are given in points, with one carat equaling 100 points.

✳ **Cut** A diamond's brilliance or sparkle is determined by the angles and proportions to which it is cut. The stone's cut is not to be confused with its shape (marquise, round, pear, etc.). Cuts have five grades: Excellent, Very Good, Good, Fair and Poor. You'll get your best bargains in the Good grade of cut. Some brilliance is forfeited for size in this category.

✳ **Clarity** The number of inclusions (flaws that are categorized as marks, cracks, chips, clouds, knots, etc.) establishes a diamond's classification: Flawless (F), Very Very Slightly Included (VVS1, 2), Very Slightly Included (VS1, 2), Slightly Included (SI1 and 2), and Included (I1, 2, 3). All rankings are determined by the visibility of the stone's flaws with 10x magnification. Stones classified SI1 and better are considered "eye clean," meaning no flaws are visible to the naked eye. Best deals are in the SI classification.

✳ **Color** The GIA's color-coding chart starts with D–F, the "colorless" ideal; G–J, almost colorless; K–M, a hint of yellow; N–R, very light yellow; and S–Z, light yellow.

Opt for a "light" carat weight. Once a diamond reaches a carat level, its price climbs, so go with a weight slightly under the carat mark you're targeting. For example, if you want a two-carat ring, shop for those at 1.9—the difference in size will be hard to notice, and you'll save. On a recent search on *pricescope.com* (a site for comparison-shopping for diamonds and other gems), a 1.9-carat diamond ranged from $8,663 to $10,490; a 2-carat from $10,120 to $11,989 (both H color; SI1).

The round brilliant-cut shape is the most costly; choose one of the "fancy" shapes—marquise, princess, oval, emerald—which are less expensive.

Very tiny differences in color or clarity can translate to big differences in price. Look at the Slight Inclusion stones, as well as K, L color grades. If the stone is "eye clean," and you love it, go for it. (Examine stone carefully and have it evaluated before purchasing.)

Something old, something new: an assortment of vintage and antique reproduction rings from Antique Jewelry Mall . From top: diamond in four-prong setting with Art Deco filigree; princess-cut diamond with heart motif setting and wheat-pattern engraving; round brilliant-cut diamond with Art Deco setting and engraved platinum ring; Retro Moderne ring from the '50s with round brilliant-cut diamond.

Use gems from family heirloom jewelry to create a new ring.

Consider buying vintage. If you and your fiancé are comfortable with a pre-owned ring that was not family-owned, try antique shops (buying from reputable dealers), or a well-regarded site like *AntiqueJewelryMall.com*, which gives GIA or EGL certificates and appraisal certificates for any diamond over .25 carats. *ArtDecoDiamonds.com* has an extensive collection of period, GIA-certified diamonds. Both sites have return policies.

Online dealers can save you 30%–40% over retail prices. Go only with established sites like *BlueNile.com* or *WhiteFlash.com*, where stones are verified and all purchases can be returned.

Want to know if you're getting a good deal? Comparison shop for the carat, cut, color, clarity and shape you want on *pricescope.com*.

Purchase a loose stone online or at a wholesaler and have it set at a local jeweler.

Want a clear stone, but diamonds are too expensive? Look at white topaz, white sapphire, white tourmaline and white aquamarine.

Consider a man-made diamond. This isn't cubic zirconia, but rather a diamond grown in a laboratory, replicating natural gem formation (placing carbon under extreme heat and varying degrees of pressure). The man-made diamonds are sometimes referred to as "cultured" (à la cultured pearls, formed when natural conditions are recreated). The optical quality of lab-created gemstones has improved tremendously over the years; only a gemologist is likely to know that Mother Nature wasn't involved in your stone's creation. (And sometimes even pros have a hard time telling.) Man-mades cost about 30% less than natural diamonds. For more information, go to *apollodiamond.com* and *gemesis.com*.

Check out moissanite—the diamond-like stone made from silicon carbon crystals involving a different process and material base than man-made or synthetic diamonds. Moissanite has a higher refractive index than diamonds and runs about $525 a carat. For information, *moissanite.com*.

Consider a synthetic stone. You can always upgrade to a real stone when it's more affordable to do so. A recent article in the *New York Post* highlighted this trend of buying mock rocks now for real gem replacements later. But with the quality of some synthetics, you may not want to trade up at a later date. *DiamondNexusLabs.com* is a source for lab-created stones.

Man-made diamonds from Apollo Diamond.

Wedding bands

Wedding bands range in price from $100 to $2,000, and can go higher depending on the intricacy of the embellishment. You'll find the best deals with silver, titanium, palladium and tungsten carbide rings.

✳ **Gold** The most common metal for wedding bands, although not as durable as other metals. And gold scratches easily. Pure gold is measured at 24 karats, with lesser percentages indicated accordingly. 18K has 75% gold, mixed with other alloys. 14K contains 58.3% gold. (Bands can also be found in 10 karat gold.) White gold is blended with silver or nickel and often plated with rhodium; rose gold is blended with copper.

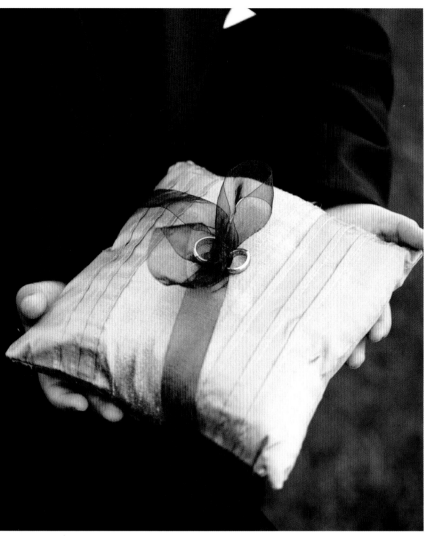

✳ **Platinum** The most expensive metal, more durable than gold. Sets off diamonds beautifully, which is why it's so popular as a wedding band material. Tarnish resistant, although it scratches easily.

✳ **Palladium** Part of the same metal family as platinum, although whiter in color and about 70% less expensive.

✳ **Sterling silver** Inexpensive, although prone to both tarnishing and scratching.

✳ **Titanium** Extremely strong (rings cannot be resized), lightweight and inexpensive. For those who don't want the shiny white of silver or platinum, the muted grays of this metal might appeal.

✳ **Tungsten carbide** The most wear-resistant material for a ring; it's indestructible, virtually scratch-proof and has a "permanent" polish. May be difficult to remove during a medical emergency.

the well-priced ring

If you want your wedding ring to look as if it belongs with your engagement ring, shop accordingly. The wedding ring should have the same band shape as the engagement ring, although slightly larger; e.g., match a straight-edge engagement ring band with a straight-edge wedding ring band. If the engagement ring has a low stone setting, or an unusually shaped band, look at curved or fitted wedding rings. The bride's and groom's rings don't have to match, but many couples like them to.

Research online for cost savings. A recent search on *BlueNile.com* turned up platinum rings for women for $245 and white gold for $210. Other sites to note: *affordableweddingbands.com, overstock.com, e-weddingbands.com.*

Jacqueline Sutej
&
Lachlan Carlyle

APR

CHAPTER 5

INVITATIONS and WEDDING STATIONERY

When it comes to sending wedding invitations, paper still rules. "Invitations set the tone for your wedding—formal, casual, the degree of creativity," says Sarah Meyer Walsh, co-owner of Haute Papier in Washington, D.C. "And you don't want to set the wrong one. A smart invitation can even tip the balance between guests wanting to attend—particularly if they're out-of-towners—and not."

While the number of wedding e-vites increased by 60%, from 750,000 to 1.2 million, in 2008 according to *Evite.com*, many brides still consider them a bit too informal.

Save the Date

Celebrate the Marriage of
Jacqueline and Aristotle
Saturday, October 20th, 1968
Skorpios, Greece

Invitation to follow

Wedding stationery 101

The wedding paper trail can be a long and pricey one, averaging $659 (for invites and reply cards) according to the Bridal Association of America. Wedding invitations run anywhere from $1 (if you do them yourself) to $10 per invite (at the ritziest stationers, for hand-engraved lettering on 120-pound card stock).

Considering an invitation is only one (although the most important) component of wedding stationery, it's easy to see how the costs can add up. Here's a full list of the items you can (but don't have to) order:

✴ Invitations (sometimes preceded by a Save-the-Date card)

✴ RSVP cards and envelopes

✴ Reception cards (if reception is held at a different site from the ceremony)

✴ Directions cards

✴ Accommodations cards (for out-of-town guests)

Above: A whimsical Save-the-Date sample from e-vite stationer Paperless Post. Right: Custom stationery designed by Atlanta graphic designer Ashley Summerlin at her studio Dolci Odille for her wedding. Opposite, top and center: A selection of Elum letterpress invitations, "Salon" and "Bone," made with soy-based inks. Opposite, bottom: Haute Papier letterpress invitation, RSVP, and seating cards.

✳ Seating cards (indicating the guest's table)

✳ Placecards (indicating the guest's seat at a specific table)

✳ Menu cards

✳ Wedding programs

Still haven't had enough? What about pew cards or rain cards (indicating the alternative site for an outdoor wedding)? And don't forget invites for engagement parties, bridal showers and rehearsal dinners, and stationery for those all-important thank-you notes. Before considering ways to save on paper costs, here are a few basics.

Printing methods for invitations Research a variety of printing styles before deciding how you want your invites to look and how much you want to spend.

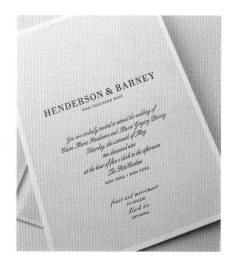

✳ **Engraving** The most expensive way to go. A metal die is cut with lettering and applied against paper, resulting in raised lettering and an indented back surface. Invitations can be hand or machine engraved.

✳ **Letterpress** As the word implies, letters are pressed deep into the paper for a fine, etched look. Ideal for heavy paper stock.

✳ **Thermography** Resin powder is added to wet ink, then heated to form raised lettering (without any reverse-side indentations as in engraving). Considerably less expensive than engraving.

✳ **Offset (lithography)** A completely flat surface—no raised lettering or indentations. The least expensive option with the exception of home printing.

✳ **Home printers** Laser or ink-jet printing provides a flat surface, laser ink giving a sharper print quality.

Paper 80–110-pound stock is commonly used for wedding invitations; 32–64-pound for ancillary wedding items. The most expensive paper is 100% cotton, which provides the smoothest surface. Linen stock is made from cotton, with a slightly textured (linen fabric-like) surface. Parchment is translucent, frequently used for calligraphy, and often attached to heavier card stock. Cotton vellum is also translucent, comes in a variety of thicknesses and, like parchment, typically attaches to heavier stock.

Invitation styles Of course, you can be creative and design your own shape, but that will require special cutting and often a custom-sized envelope.

✳ **Single panel** One page of stock, typically measuring 5¼"–5½" x 7½"–7¾". As it is only one sheet, it usually takes the heaviest stock. Often has a raised border.

❧ SOURCES:
DIY Invitations

DICKBLICK.COM For a wide selection of paper types, colors and styles, as well as artists' supplies.

DO-IT-YOURSELF-INVITATIONS. COM Free templates, card-making instructions. Custom templates from $10.

EARTHINVITATIONS.COM offers DIY lotka wedding kits with recycled tree-free, vegetable-dyed papers. The seed-embedded overlay paper can be printed in your home ink-jet or laser printer.

ED-IT.COM ED/iT's *The Complete Wedding Publisher* software, $29.95, offers options for almost any type of wedding stationery: invitations, RSVP cards, menus, programs. Has a try-before-buy download option.

ENVELOPPERINC.COM A paper and software resource. Wide range of invitation styles—18 different pocket-folds, 3 gatefold styles and pochettes.

LCIPAPER.COM Wedding invitation papers, precut cards, vellum, craft supplies.

MYGATSBY.COM Paper supplies kits for DIY invites. About 17 different kits, including blank stock invitations, outer envelopes and enclosure cards, starting at $1.59 per invite. 80–110-pound stock.

PAPER-SOURCE.COM Colorful range of papers for the DIY-er; how-to videos, as well as custom wedding stationery.

UNIQUITYINVITATIONS.COM Template collections for invitations; RSVP, table and place cards; favor tags, menus and programs. From $79.

Opposite: Pocket invitation with reply card and wedding stationery from Envelopper Inc., which you can print yourself.

* **Bifold** A booklet-style invitation with a blank cover, measuring 5½" x 7¾" when folded, 11" x 7¾" when not.

* **Trifold** Here it gets interesting, with such options as Z-folds, purse-folds and gatefolds. A Z-fold has three sections of (usually) equal sizes folded vertically; purse-folds fold horizontally; gatefolds are when both edges of the invitation meet in the center.

* **Royal style** A 7" x 7" square.

How to save on wedding stationery

Do it yourself. Making your own stationery can save big money, but the cost will come in the time you spend in its production. And then you have to address all those envelopes! To determine whether this is something you want to take on, consider:

* **"If you're craft-savvy** and have worked with paper before, then go for it," says Haute Papier's Sarah Meyer Walsh. "Buy the blank card stock and design what you want. If you're not craft savvy, use one of the software kits. It will have everything you need, the right software, a range of fonts and design templates, and instructions. It's hard for the average person to design a good-looking invitation in Word. That's why you should have design software."

* **Keep in mind there are two types of invitation kits.** The software kits, with prices starting at $29.99, are for designing the invitation. The paper kits provide a blank stationery collection of everything from the invite and envelope to all the paper items (*see list, pages 60–61*) you might want before and after your wedding.

* **If you are making your invitations,** you'll need a good paper cutter for the best, most professional results. (And watch those fingers!)

* **Many home printers can't handle envelopes** or heavier paper stock. But if you still want to do the invites yourself, you can take or send your templates (and paper) to a copy shop or Kinko's to print out.

* **Search online for well-priced papers.** If you can't find the paper stock you want in a bricks-and-mortar store, check out LCI Paper (*lcipaper.com*), or Dick Blick Art Materials (*dickblick.com*).

* **DIY online.** Some sites offer one-stop shopping: Design a card or modify an existing one, then buy the supplies on the same site (*123print.com* or *lcipaper. com*). Make sure to get a sample of the stock with printing before you order.

invitations and wedding stationery

❧ SOURCES:
Ordering Stationery Online

EINVITE.COM A wide range of traditional and contemporary stationery designs, some with matching Web templates. Easy-to-use preview technology lets you instantly create a proof of your invite. Single-panel thermography styles as low as $84/100, with inner envelopes and tissues included. Samples available and liberal return policy.

FINESTATIONERY.COM Over 1,000 wedding invitation options, starting at $34/100. Unprinted stock available for the DIY-er. Detailed product descriptions. Competitive pricing on top brands.

INVITATIONHOTLINE.COM About 25% off list price of many major stationery brands.

REAVESENGRAVING.COM Very competitive prices on engraving; $145.50 for 100 classic wedding invitations on 80-pound paper.

REXCRAFT.COM Reasonably priced printed invitations, as well as card stock if you want to print your own.

✻ If you don't like any of the invitations you see in-store or online, have a template designed for you (at *do-it-yourself-invitations.com*) for a small fee, then print from your own computer, at a copy shop or Kinko's.

SCP

The honor of your presence is requested
at the reaffirmation of wedding vows of

Sara & Peter Cerulia

on Saturday, the seventeenth of February
Two thousand and nine
at six o'clock in the evening

Hilltop Manor
3 Oceanview Road
Hopetown, Elbow Cay

Dinner Reception to follow

Right and opposite: Three styles of wedding invitations from *MyGatsby.com*: the pochette-style "Bloom"; three-layer panel "Reagan"; a vertical folio pocket option with starfish embellishment. All are 5" x 7."

invitations and wedding stationery

Buying stationery

✻ **When working with stationers:** "Be upfront about the budget you can really work with, even underestimate it a bit," says Erin Miller of Haute Papier. "See what package they can come up with to get your business."

✻ **Comparison shop.** You'll find great deals online, but always get a product sample first. Pay for a full proof (not just a PDF proof) as well. The best pricing will be with predesigned cards that allow for some customization.

✻ **Put your money into your invitation** (letterpress or engraving, the thickest stock), using less expensive papers and printing methods for ancillary items.

✻ **The single-panel invite in a traditional size** (5½" x 7¾") with just an outer envelope will be the least expensive to order. And to mail.

✻ **Order extra invitations.** Many planners recommend having at least 20–30 spare invitations and 30–40 extra envelopes to allow for changes in the guest list and mistakes while addressing. Include the overage when you first place your order; it will be cheaper than if you have to go back to the printer for extras.

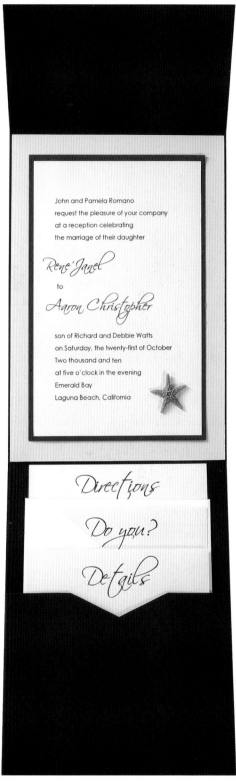

What you can forgo

✳ **The invitation envelope** into which the invitation is placed before slipping into the addressing envelope.

✳ **Envelope linings and tissue overlays** add to the final bill and could add extra postage costs, too.

✳ **RSVP cards** Set up RSVPs to your wedding website (*see page 68*) or simply have guests reply by phone. If you want an inexpensive RSVP card, create a postcard in a stock that's complementary to your invitation. No need for envelopes, and the postage will be less than for a first-class letter.

✳ **Direction cards and maps** Create your own for free at *weddingmapper. com* or post on your wedding website.

✳ **Accommodations cards** Add this information to your website or send out an e-mail blast to your guests.

When your invitations are completed, take one to the post office to see what the exact postage requirements will be.

If you want to go modern with an e-vite, check out *paperlesspost. com*. Here, you'll find gorgeous e-vites that look as beautiful and detailed as offerings from the poshest paper stationers. The site also allows you to track all of your invitations and see who has accepted, declined and even opened your invite. *Evite.com* has templates for free wedding invitations, in addition to budget calculators and other party planning tools.

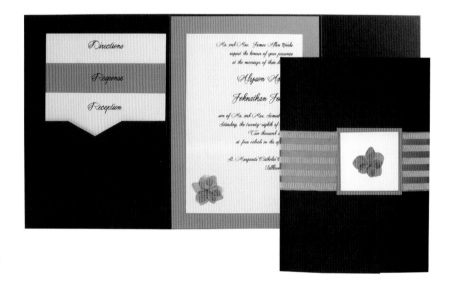

This page: From *MyGatsby.com*, a jacket-style, above, and right, a gate folio pocket invite; both are 5" x 7." Opposite: "Pewter" pocket invitation with seal from Envelopper Inc. Seals are home-printer compatible.

Personal wedding websites

A personal wedding website can save a tremendous amount of hassle, time and money. While you may or may not be ready for e-vites, posting just about any type of wedding information on your site makes sense for the savvy, time-starved couple. So with a little e-planning, you and your fiancé won't have to be fielding last-minute calls on everything from weather to driving directions.

WHAT THESE SITES CAN DO FOR YOU

✻ Help coordinate all events preceding the actual wedding: engagement party, bridal showers, bachelor and bachelorette parties, rehearsal dinners.

✻ Manage RSVPS to the wedding ceremony and reception.

✻ Create a wedding e-mail list for updates about the wedding after invitations have been sent out.

✻ Coordinate travel options for out-of-town guests (hotels, car rentals, restaurants near hotel where guests are staying), as well as alert them to any discounts the couple has been able to arrange for accommodations during their stay.

✻ Link to local weather sites.

✻ For destination weddings, help organize everyone's travel plans, arrival and departure dates and times, hotel bookings, transportation to and from airports.

✻ Create a wedding biography of the bride and groom.

✻ Provide mini-bios of the bridal party, parents of the bride and groom, and members of respective families for guests.

✻ Post photos of all pre-wedding activities.

✻ Get an opinion: Can't decide on the wedding site/menu/color scheme? Post pix of a few choices and get feedback from family and guests.

✻ Post lunch or dinner menu options, if you are providing them, and allow guests to register their preferences.

✻ Provide a calendar for all wedding-related events, which then can be updated with time changes and locations (in the case of bad weather for outdoor venues).

✻ Link to gift registry or registries.

invitations and wedding stationery

* Link to interactive maps.

* In some instances, online design templates can be coordinated with your stationery (*mywedding.com*).

* Host a blog.

* Serve as an e-guestbook for guests who attend the wedding and for those who can't, allowing them to post best wishes and thoughts on the site.

* After the wedding, link to photographer's online gallery for family to purchase pictures.

* Can include slide shows and other photo album options.

* Allow guests to upload pictures they took at the wedding for all to see.

* Allow wedding videos to be uploaded.

* Allow for post-wedding updates.

KEEP IN MIND

* **Most hosting sites,** whether free or fee-based, allow you to develop a trial site before creating a final one. Try out a few to see if you'll get the design and features you want, if you have an easy time creating and navigating the site, and whether you'll have enough photo storage capacity.

* **As soon as you're engaged, set up the site**—even if it's just a single page. You can then list the website on your Save-the-Date cards.

* **With free hosting sites,** check to see if any ads will be appearing on your personal site (sometimes just visible to you, not your guests), and what, if any, features might involve fees.

* **With free sites, you'll get a personal address on their domain.** See if you can establish your own domain name—it generally doesn't cost that much per month to do so.

* **Fee-based sites range from $25 to over $200 per year,** depending on hosting capabilities. Most allow a 7–14-day free trial. Minimum hosting times vary from one to 12 months, so check what yours will require. Maximum hosting time ranges from 12 months to forever. With most fee-based providers, you'll be given anywhere from six to an unlimited number of pages for your site. (Extra fees often apply if you exceed the maximum page allotment for your plan and if you want additional services.) The number of page templates offered on the best-known sites range from a half-dozen to hundreds. Check out reader reviews of wedding website providers at *weddingwebsites.com*

FREE SITES
Ewedding.com
Momentville.com
Mywedding.com
Weddingwire.com

FEE-BASED SITES
Weddingorg.com
Weddingwindow.com
Wedpagedesigns.com
Wedshare.com
Wedsimple.com

CHAPTER 6

AFFORDABLE RECEPTIONS

Even with careful planning, receptions, which typically take up about 35% of a wedding budget, can quickly turn into a money pit. While the average cost of a wedding reception runs about $12,300 according to The Wedding Report, that number can be much higher in major cities.

So how do you celebrate the first moments of your marriage in style while keeping costs in line? In this chapter, top wedding planners, caterers, wine experts, and design and lighting pros tell you how.

Generally, rehearsal dinners are limited to the wedding party and immediate families, but once the guest list expands (sometimes to include out-of-town guests), costs can get out of control. Here's how to keep an eye on the bottom line.

HAVE A LUNCH before the rehearsal instead of a dinner.

HOLD THE DINNER AT A CHINESE RESTAURANT or family-style Italian restaurant.

IN GOOD WEATHER, HOST A BARBECUE. It can be held at the groom's parents' house or a friend's house, depending on where the groom and the couple's friends live.

PLAN A COCKTAIL PARTY INSTEAD OF A LUNCH OR DINNER. Rehearsal dinners are all about toasting the couple, the families, etc., so a cocktails-only event is ideal.

* **Reduce the guest list.** It can be painful deciding who makes the cut, but the discomfort from a whopping reception bill will be even greater. Take your scissors to the guest list early and stay firm.

* **Have a two-part celebration.** The day of your wedding, hold a small reception for your nearest and dearest (under 25 people). After the honeymoon, host a more casual affair—a cocktail party, for example—where you invite friends, extended family and work colleagues.

* **Marry off-season.** With weddings, timing is everything. Since roughly 70% of weddings take place between May and October, you can see why event spaces and vendors might be eager for your business at other times of the year. And this eagerness can turn into discounts of 30% to 40% or more. There are other advantages: You're likely to get more attention from your vendors, e.g., your caterer or your photography crew, during a slow time than if you were to marry in June, when bookings are at their highest. Here's what to keep in mind:

◆ Off-season varies in different parts of the country. August may be a peak month in Maine, much less so in Florida (hurricane season!). If you're in doubt, check with hotels and event spaces about their down times; particularly important when you're planning a destination wedding and aren't familiar with the seasonal quirks of a locale. (March, hardly a month northern brides associate with peak season, can be prime in a warm-weather climate.)

◆ Some "off" months are better than others. While the slowest month for weddings is December, event spaces (at least when the economy was good) get booked for holiday and charity parties, and might not be able to offer significant discounts. February is an off month in most parts of the country, except for Valentine's Day and the week leading up to it.

* **Brush up those negotiating skills.** First, comparison shop for sites, caterers, bands and photographers. Remember when you were applying to college and had a "safe" school? For wedding planning, have "safe" vendors—those you can fall back on if you can't strike better deals. Your bargaining power and leverage increases when you have a plan B. Ask prospective vendors politely but firmly, *Is that your best offer? I was hoping for a lower price*. "And if you don't get the answer you want the first time from a vendor, arrange to speak to someone else at the company," says Sarah Doheny of Sarah's Events and Bridal (*sarahseventsandbridal.com*), a Pennsylvania-based event-planning company. "You may be dealing with a 'newbie' who doesn't know what can be done."

* **Consider a destination wedding.** Seems counterintuitive to try to save money by holding your wedding far from home. Since not everyone will want, can afford, or can take the time to travel to Cancun or St. Thomas with you, guest lists tend to shrink. And if you can plan your festivities to take place between Sunday and Thursday, the "slow" days at most resorts, you might benefit from some considerable discounts.

* **Or at least get out of town.** Hold the ceremony and reception outside a large city. With a 30- to 60-minute drive away from a major metropolitan area, the pricing can be far more attractive. For example (and this is a high-end one), if you were to hold a sit-down dinner at the Ritz-Carlton on Central Park South in New York, the per-person cost is $295 to $350. Go to the Ritz-Carlton in White Plains in nearby Westchester County, and you can (if you do a lunch) get that down to $100 per person (all exclusive of taxes and gratuities).

Before a reception at the Copamarina Beach Resort and Spa in Puerto Rico.

If you need to marry during a peak wedding month, you can still find ways to keep costs down.

✳ **Don't marry on a Saturday night.** That's wedding party prime time. If you want a sit-down dinner, you'll get better prices for a Friday (schedule so guests have time to arrive from work) or Sunday night wedding. Consider a Thursday evening, which in some cities is being called "the new Friday" (which was once "the new Saturday") for wedding dinners.

✳ **Still have your heart set on a peak-season Saturday event?** "A Saturday sit-down lunch can cost a third less than a dinner only a few hours later," says Julia Erlichman of Julia & Friends Event Management, a Philadelphia-based event planning company. "The menu will be very similar to the dinner menu, but at a much better price." And with lunch, you can forgo the band and dancing, which will save money as well.

✳ **Buffets aren't always the most cost effective.** A sit-down dinner with a fixed menu (and allowances for vegetarian or special diets) can be easier on your budget than a multi-stationed top-line buffet. Strategize with the caterer or chef you'll be hiring. He or she will know what's in season and how to plan the best menu for your dollar.

✳ **Let's do brunch/breakfast.** Wedding planners recommend brunches for the bride looking for a stylish way to entertain guests without an exorbitant price tag.

A brunch will be less costly than a lunch at your chosen venue, and you'll save on liquor costs, too. And guests who have to travel a distance will be eternally grateful that they don't have to book another hotel night! Sunrise ceremony anyone? (It's sometimes considered a mischievous way to cut down a guest list.) If you and your fiancé are early risers, opt for a wedding breakfast (a favorite of British royals), which will run about the same or be slightly less expensive than a brunch. And with a breakfast fête, you can head to your honeymoon destination that much sooner.

✳ **Sweet-talk.** The all-dessert reception is basically an update of the Champagne and cake celebration that once was the standard postnuptial party. Generally scheduled between 3 and 5 p.m., with Champagne and signature cocktails.

✳ **Have a cocktail reception.** Typically held between 5 and 7 p.m., the hors d'oeuvres and drinks party is best scheduled for a non-workday, so guests can arrive in time.

Left: Trout caviar on a brioche star by Mary Cleaver of The Cleaver Company.

Secrets from top wedding planners

BETH HELMSTETTER, owner of Beth Helmstetter Events in Los Angeles (*bethhelmstetter.com*); 818-238-7070

✻ **Think small:** I encourage my clients to go for a smaller wedding. It allows for a more intimate experience.

✻ **Off-peak favorites:** I'm a big fan of Friday-night cocktail reception parties, which can be a lot of fun. I also like dessert receptions, with Champagne and mimosas on a Sunday afternoon.

✻ **It's all in the details:** With tight budgets, I recommend focusing on the small touches that can enhance a wedding's style. For example, if the ceremony is outdoors, we'll hand out iced teas in pretty glasses to guests as they arrive. We'll have an assortment of pashminas in a rainbow of colors available if we expect the weather to be a bit windy or chilly. We keep parasols for sun protection in chic wicker baskets. We arrange placecards on silver trays and place rose petals between the rows.

✳ **Tablescapes:** I prefer a long table to numerous smaller ones; it's more dramatic. Alternate bouquets of hydrangeas—you get a lot of flower for the cost—with groupings of candles. Alternate roses in small square vases with votives. I like to use this combination as a "runner" on a long banquet table. I also recommend renting the best table and chair linens you can afford. Good quality linens will let you get away with fewer decorations.

✳ **Write stuff:** I'm into calligraphy—placecards, menus and programs can be designed inexpensively and provide a great decorative touch at the reception site.

✳ **Five-star hotel "find":** A five-star hotel or resort's banquet room may be beyond your budget, but check out their restaurants and see if they have a private room. You'll get a great reception location and often a lower per-person meal cost.

✳ **The last-minute wedding:** If your lead time is less than two months, you might be able to get an incredible deal. The sooner the event, the better the cost savings might be. Negotiate aggressively. The site knows it's unlikely another last-minute event will come along and should be eager for your business.

Opposite: Tablescape and buffet table, Beth Helmstetter Events. Above: Placecards in bloom, Beth Helmstetter Events. Left: All white table decor from BBJ Linen.

LORI STEPHENSON, owner
of Lola Event Productions
(*lolaeventproductions.com*), cited by
Chicago magazine as one of the top
wedding event companies in the city

Above: Focus on presentation style to
maximize your catering budget.
Opposite: Tablescape at the Olympic Sculpture
Park in Seattle, a popular site for weddings.

✳ **Brunches are your best cost saver.** If you want to have a classy, unique event with style, without the attendant price tag, this is what I tell my clients to do. You can save 40%–50% of what dinner would cost at the same venue. Limit liquor choices to mimosas, Bloody Marys and wine—I haven't had any complaints when we suggest this. Depending on the venue, a brunch can run from 11:30 to 4, in which case the usage cost per hour adds up to a tremendous deal.

✳ **Focus on presentation.** Stylish food presentation can make your budget seem larger than it is and add to your reception's "wow" factor. We recently sampled a fabulous appetizer served on a chic rectangular plate with small-portion slots for a salad, a shot glass of soup, and a serving of bruschetta with mozzarella. It looked fabulous and nothing was expensive. See if your caterer has stylish, modern plates, interesting rectangulars and squares, colored chargers and unusual appetizer plates—or if he or she can rent them.

✳ **Don't overlook serving pasta as an entrée.** It's gentle on the budget. Innovative new pastas will please the vegans in the crowd and can make for great displays of color and texture. Stuffed pastas are the easiest to prepare and serve. For fall, perhaps a ravioli with squash filling; in spring, an artichoke lasagna.

✳ **Better to serve good-quality chicken than poor-quality steak.** Again, a good caterer can suggest how to cook and present your entrée in a modern, stylish way.

✳ **Table design:** Go with candles. Vary their heights and widths. In many places, the law requires candles to be in glass containers, so these can add interest to the tablescape. Do the floating candle business. Submerge an orchid bloom in a vase. Contrast table runners.

✳ **Sites:** Try to pick a site that you like enough so you don't have to spend a lot of money decorating to transform it. And think out of the box. A new favorite wedding venue in Chicago is a flower shop/event space called A New Leaf.

✳ **Reception decor:** I love flowers, but there can be real sticker shock when you estimate the cost to decorate with them. Use lighting to create a mood instead. Simple uplights to highlight architectural details and interesting gobos will do a lot to create the ambiance you want. With the right lighting, you can get away with a much simpler decor.

✳ **Don't spend money on things you're not excited about** just because there's a tradition behind them—for example, if you don't want a cake, don't go to the expense of having one. A client who loved strawberry shortcake had a shortcake bar where guests could help themselves to variations on this classic.

LEANA GALLAGHER, owner and president of The Events and Occasions Company, with branches in Manhattan, New England, the Southwest and Amelia Island (*manhattanoccasions. com, newenglandoccasions. com, southwestoccasions.com, ameliaoccasions.com*)

✳ **Save on a sit-down dinner.** Think protein first, starch second. Have your expensive items, like shrimp shooters, or a crostini with tenderloin and arugula, as hors d'oeuvres. For entrées, perhaps a risotto with ham and peas. Or if you really need to have a meat entrée, consider pork. It's less predictable and about the same cost as chicken, easy to serve, and works well with sweet and savory sauces.

✳ **BYOB.** Try to select a venue where you can supply your own liquor; it will save scads of money, costing about $15 per person as opposed to $50 per person at a traditional venue. For a 100-guest party, the liquor should run about $2,000. (Figure $1,500 for the liquor and $300–$500 for the bartender and tips.)

✳ **Keep an open bar throughout your party.** Let's face it, liquor makes a party. This is one area where I don't recommend cost cutting. An open bar can actually be more cost effective than a wine and single special-cocktail service. Figure you get four glasses out of a bottle of $30 wine and eight out of a $30 bottle of vodka or other liquor.

✳ **Cake costs are easy to control:** Go with a supermarket cake, or one made by your local bakery, and you'll get the average cost per serving down to $3. If you live in the South, the supermarket chain Publix (*publix.com*) has a selection of reasonably priced wedding cakes from which to choose.

✳ **When buying flowers:** Since in-season flowers will save you money, ask your florist what will be available for your wedding day. The best deals might not be for the types of flowers blooming in your backyard at the time of your wedding. They'll be for the flowers that are available to florists, usually from South America. And don't overlook the inexpensive carnation. This flower can look quite beautiful in bouquets and can be worked into wonderful topiary.

✳ **Tablescapes:** A quick and easy one is with roses and small square-glass votive holders. Cut stems from roses; place one bud in each of the glass holders. Arrange 12 of the holders to create a solid square. Place along the length of a banquet table (every 4 feet or so), or center one on each guest table (create a larger square depending on table size). Trim with Spanish moss. Other ideas: Buy clear cylinder vases and float an orchid or orchid stem in each. Or submerge orchids or orchid stems in clear vases filled with water.

✳ **Rent beautiful candelabra and fill with long tapers.** Place one per round table, or spaced along a banquet-style table. Hurricane lamps with pillar candles surrounded by flowers or greens are also lovely. As some sites won't allow lit candles, go with battery-operated ones. They'll look fine.

* **What's considered high and low season can vary** among states within a region. For example, August is a peak wedding month in Boston, but less popular in New York City. November is an off month most everywhere, but not Santa Fe. March is high season in Florida, but less so in many other Southern states. Know what you'll be dealing with if you're not wedding in your hometown.

* **Favorite good-value venues:** The Ribault Club (*theribaultclub.com*, rates from $1,250) in Jacksonville, Florida, run by the National Park Service, and the Commandant's House (*commandantshouse.com*, rates from $1,225) in Boston, also run by the National Parks.

Above, clockwise from top left: the Ribault Club gardens, an interior shot of the Club, a wedding menu.

CHRISTIAN O'DOWD, owner,
The Cantering Caterer
(*canteringcaterer.com*), based in
Westport, Connecticut; 203-227-2208

✳ **Saving on reception costs:**
Flavorful, seasonal food needn't be
expensive, and if imaginatively
prepared, no one questions the
budget. For entrées, if you want
steak, I'd suggest a roulade with
Swiss chard, mushrooms and Piave
Vecchio cheese. For pastas, serve
with seasonal sautéed vegetables.
In spring, I'd recommend a
combination of asparagus,
prosciutto, shaved Pecorino Romano,
and fiddlehead ferns. For fall, a mix
of vegetables—thinly sliced purple
and golden beets, turnips, butternut
squash, served with pumpkin
fettuccine (easy to make). Choose
a flavorful, unexpected appetizer
like dates stuffed with goat cheese,
wrapped in bacon.

✳ **Cake:** You can save hundreds of
dollars by having a two-tier cake
for cutting, then cupcakes, either to
match the cake or contrast with it.
If you want a full-blown lavishly
decorated cake, go to a local
culinary school. They have
pastry and bakery departments, and
students often need photos of their
work for their portfolios. They might
be able to knock something out of
the park for you. Of course, have a
test run and sample first.

affordable receptions

* **Reasonably priced sites:**
The Waveny House, a beautiful old-stone mansion in New Canaan, Connecticut; 203-594-3600 (from $1,500 for 10-hour usage). The banquet halls at Penfield Beach in Fairfield, Connecticut, have spacious indoor facilities right on the water (from $500 for residents, $950 for nonresidents, plus fee for police officer. *fairfieldrecreation.com/ penfield rentals.html*; 203-256-3144). Burr Homestead (*fairfieldhs.org/rent- burr-homestead*; 203-522-4629), an 18th-century Greek Revival–style mansion, also in Fairfield (from $350).

* **Tabletop:** Instead of having to pay for a table overlay, invest in nicely textured linens. For the centerpiece, use tinted votives with candles in different sizes and shapes.

* **Liquor:** Limit liquor to Champagne and wine, or wine and (in summer) one mixed drink. Since 80% of mixed drinks consumed in warm-weather months are vodka-based, I would go with vodka for the liquor choice. Why pay for a bottle of Scotch when only one guest might order it?

* **Bargain Champagne:** I like Charles de Fère's Champagne blend, about $10 to $12 a bottle.

MARY CLEAVER, founder and owner of The Cleaver Company (*cleaverco. com*; 75 9th Ave., NYC; 212-741-9174), a pioneer in the sustainable food movement, with A-list and top corporate clients, talks about how to have a fabulous reception menu at a reasonable price.

Above: Cupcakes have become an increasingly popular and affordable alternative to pricey wedding cakes. Right, top: Catering guru Mary Cleaver suggests a soup first course using seasonal ingredients, as in this gazpacho, to save on reception costs. Right: For a cocktail-party reception, hors d'oeuvres needn't be expensive, like the poached figs served here. Opposite: Try to choose a venue where you can provide your own liquor.

A CELEBRITY CATERER'S TIPS

✳ **For New Yorkers looking to save on reception costs,** I would recommend a cocktail party. A brunch would be my second choice. I've not seen too many requests for breakfasts, but that may be because New York is a city that runs late. A lot of popular event sites in New York City are on the West Side, designed to take advantage of evening sunsets, so that's another reason I recommend cocktail parties.

affordable receptions

✳ **For a memorable cocktail party,** ask your caterer to come up with imaginative hors d'oeuvres that reflect the season. I like soup shots, onion and goat cheese tartlets, poached figs, vegetable tarts. None of the ingredients need be expensive.

✳ **For sit-downs,** a soup first course is the most economical, particularly when using seasonal vegetables. Make it interesting: Depending on the season, a spring pea or parsnip soup, maybe a gazpacho.

✳ **For entrées,** mahi can be reasonable. I'd wrap it in a banana leaf and serve with passion fruit vinaigrette. Chicken potpies are another option.

✳ **For pasta as an entrée** (you wouldn't have a soup first course), I'd recommend lasagna—something that can be prebaked and reheated, which is important if you're at an untraditional site. Ask your caterer for an unusual pasta combination, like a tricolor lasagna or an herbed-pasta rotolo with spinach and ricotta filling.

✳ **For reception wines, stay local.** If you're near a wine-growing region, you can find some great deals. For those in or near the New York metropolitan area, two Long Island vintners offering good value are Macari with Merlots starting at $11 a bottle and Wölffer Estate with rosés about $16 per bottle.

✳ **Keep cake costs down with cupcakes.** You can have a lot of fun with the cake/icing combinations depending on the season. For spring, I'd recommend a buttermilk cake with lemon buttercream icing; for fall, gingerbread with maple meringue.

How to save on reception liquor costs

✳ **Champagne has the highest cost per serving** of any alcoholic beverage, so you may want to consider limiting it to the cake-cutting toast.

✳ **Instead of Champagne, serve a well-priced sparkling wine.** If jeroboams of Krug are a bit beyond your budget, consider what the pros at Sherry-Lehmann and Morrell, two of New York City's finest liquor and wine emporiums, recommend for Champagne substitutes (*right*).

✳ **Restrict the open bar** to the pre-reception hour or hours; serve wine and nonalcoholic beverages at the actual reception.

✳ **The savings will be considerable** if a venue allows you to provide your own liquor. Hire a bartender, plan with him or her what you'll need, and purchase the liquor yourself from a store with a buy-back policy.

KIMBERLY MALLARD at Sherry-Lehmann (*sherry-lehmann.com*) suggests for international sparkling wines: Jaume Serra Cristalino Brut Cava (a *Wine Spectator* favorite), $7.95; Zardetto Prosecco, $12.95; Louis Bouillot Crémant de Bourgogne Grande Reserve NV, $12.95. For American sparkling wines: Roederer Estate Brut NV (made by the same folks that make Cristal), $18.95; Domaine Carneros Brut NV (by Taittinger), $19.95.

THOMAS STANLEY, wine consultant at Morrell (*morrellwine.com*), suggests among international sparking wines: Paul Cheneau Cava, from $12; Riondo Prosecco, $13; Codorníu Cava, from $15; Nino Franco "Rustico" Prosecco, about $18. For American sparkling wines: Gruet Champagnes (from New Mexico), from $15; Scharffenberger Champagnes (from California), from $17.

Decorating for value and style

Chic wedding decor in four (relatively easy) steps.

1 **Tables:** Rent as many 72" round tables as you will need (a 72" round will sit 10). Cover with ivory, floor-length tablecloths. If your budget permits, add a tulle overlay. Rent white chair covers (for folding chairs); cover with a tulle swag. Or rent gold or white ballroom chairs; you won't need additional chair covers.

2 **Create tablescapes made with pillar candles** of varying heights and widths (check on the venue's open-flame policy), centered on a white square or rectangular tray. Greenery trim optional. Other low-cost (non-flower) centerpieces can be created from wineglass shades, even decorative birdcages.

3 **Make your napkin an interesting part of the tablescape** with a special fold. (For ideas, go to *millikentablelinen.com.*)

4 **Position paper lanterns**—square paper or oval shades in white, ivory or whatever color goes with your wedding scheme— across the ceiling at your reception site. "Vary heights and dimensions," suggests event lighting specialist Melanie Lewis, manager at *PartyLights.com.* "Or create a canopy of string lights over the venue ceiling for a star-studded effect. Wrap string lights around columns, or weave through topiaries for extra glittery touches."

Left: Tie chair covers in interesting ways for a low-cost decorative touch. Covers from BBJ Linen.

TWO DECORATING PROS ON CREATING STYLISH ENVIRONMENTS

Recommendations from **JAN CANCILA,** president of Houston-based The Linen House (*linenhouse.com*); 877-522-1711

❋ **Use color for impact.** It will make your decorating budget seem more lavish. For example, if your venue only provides basic white tablecloths (make sure they reach to the floor), rent colorful overlays and napkins. Chair covers with color sashes (sometimes more than one) are easy ways to add low-cost color accents.

❋ **An interesting knot treatment for the tablecloth hem** or chair covers can provide no-cost decorative touches.

❋ **Consider an embroidered cloth,** faille or even upholstery fabric instead of the more traditional organza or chiffon for a visually interesting table overlay.

❋ **Centerpiece ideas:** A 14 x 14 solid square of 2" votives provides a high-impact tablescape at a fraction of the cost of flowers. Use a mirrored tray as a base for enhanced lighting effects. Birch branches (sometimes sprayed white, silver or gold) with clear or white string lights or with submersible Floralytes (which can be placed in water and last for six to eight hours) also look great.

❋ **Square versus round tables?** I like the impact you get from the mix of shapes. The preference is sometimes regional. For a while in Los Angeles, 60" x 60" square tables seating eight were big; in Houston, rounds were most popular.

❋ **Opt for the slightly larger table, whether square or round.** So instead of seating eight, you seat 10 to 12. Cuts down slightly on rental costs for tables and accessories, and costs for centerpieces.

Below: A reception at the Seattle Asian Art Museum.

Decorating tips from **BILL PRY**, co-owner of Chicago-based BBJ Linen (*bbjlinen.com*)

Below and opposite: A "mod" table setting created by Courtney Keefe de Jauregui, of Flush Designs.

♪ SOURCES:
Party Rentals

Companies with linens, table and chair coverings that ship nationwide. All include helpful sizing charts.

BBJ LINEN (*bbjlinen.com*) For couples who are into color, there are numerous up-to-the-minute choices within each color palette—including over 35 ivories! Design advice and a range of chair cover styles.

LINEN EFFECTS (*lineneffects.com*) Designer Collections photos show complete table settings and cost per person, from $4.85.

THE LINEN HOUSE (*linenhouse. com*) This firm makes its own linens and offers a great range of fabrics, textures and pattern styles. Exquisite embroidered organza overlays, even some toiles. Chair covers include fitted, self-tie, and sheer organzas. Helpful instruction guides for how to tie that chair sash or decorative knot.

✳ **Keep the styling simple if you're on a budget.** The centerpiece could be a bouquet of tulips in a clear round bowl. You pick up the color of the tulips in your tablecloth and go with a contrasting tone for the napkins. It doesn't have to be more elaborate than that.

✳ **"Out-there" colors like cerise are harder to make work on a budget.** They need the softeners of flowers and interesting table decor.

✳ **Linens in "fashion colors" are available at every price point,** so you can get a modern feel to your reception decor even if you have little to spend.

✳ **Use accents to punch up reception decor.** If your venue only has basic white tablecloths, bring the room to life with color accents for napkins, overlays and chair sashes, which can be rented inexpensively.

✳ **Recent popular color combinations:** Apple-green and gray; purples and pinks. Use a gray tablecloth with apple-green napkins, reversed for the bride-and-groom and display tables. Muted purple tablecloths with pink champagne napkins, reversed for the display and bride-and-groom tables. Overlays, chair coverings and sashes can extend the scheme.

A DIY LOW-COST CENTERPIECE *(left)*

A '60s-inspired "mod" table setting, created by Courtney Keefe de Jauregui, who owns Flush Designs, a custom invitation and event-planning company, first shown on *OnceWed.com*.

"I wanted the table to have a mid-century Paris feel," Keefe says. To stay within a small budget and not have the flowers be the main focus, Keefe chose streamlined modern vases for small groupings of flowers. "I started with the basics—round table, white tablecloth, black napkins and basic white dishes—all items that most venues supply. I added torn strips of striped fabric to make runners so it wasn't an all-white table, and added pattern plates on top of the white dishes to brighten them a bit. In keeping with the '60s theme, I used old records, a vintage camera, and candy cigarettes. For additional decorative touches, flowers were added to espresso cups and martini glasses were filled with Lemon Drops to add a splash of color. Balloons with escort cards tied with pink ribbon can be used to guide guests to their tables."

MATERIALS

FABRIC from Jo-Ann Fabrics

PINK PLATES from Anthropologie

CANDY CIGARETTES from *OldTimeCandy.com*

VASES from Ikea

RECORDS from a variety of Goodwills

VINTAGE TWIN LENS CAMERA from Keefe's collection

GLASSES and **CUPS** from Anthropologie, Pottery Barn, and Ikea.

INVITATIONS, ESCORT CARDS and **TABLE NUMBERS** designed and printed by Keefe

FLOWERS from the Los Angeles Flower Mart: orchids, stock, freesia, ranunculus

---

✳ **With the site decor, not every color has to be an exact match.** Trying to find table linens in the exact blue of your attendants' gowns can be the cause of a lot of unnecessary stress unless you're doing custom. Stay within a color family and you should be fine.

✳ **Chair covers:** For them to work (and be worth the rental cost), they have to fit and be installed properly.

✳ **Know your site.** Couples use the Internet to do most of their wedding research, but you really need to inspect your site before determining the reception decor. Try to see the venue when it's set up for an event. Think of how your color scheme is going to play across the room. Don't try to match your colors to the carpet. Tables are going to cover most of the rug and it won't be visible when the lights go down. Too many brides get hung up on the venue's rug color instead of focusing on the palette they want.

The well-priced cake

Wedding cakes run between $1.50 and $10 (sometimes more) a slice, the higher pricing for the elaborate, multi-tiered, fondant-swathed extravaganzas you see in so many bridal magazines. Assuming you're going with a cake, here's how to save:

✳ **Your cake needs only one "real" tier,** which will be the one you cut. The other tiers can be dummies (usually Styrofoam covered with icing). Ask your baker for an additional "kitchen," or sheet, cake to serve guests—it will have the same cake and icing, but without the elaborate decorations, so your cost per serving will be less.

✳ **Venues often charge a cutting fee** if a cake is brought in from an outside vendor, so total up the charges (plus the usual $50 to $100 delivery and cake assembly fee) to see how cost effective it really will be if you don't go with the venue's baker.

✳ **Square cakes allow for more slices than round cakes** of the same dimension, so you may want to consider this less traditional and more modern shape.

✳ **Cake toppings can be expensive.** Use real (nontoxic) flowers or look for inexpensive gum-paste decorations from an online cake decorating supplier (*see right*).

✳ **As our wedding planners advised,** go with cupcakes (or even mini-cakes and cookies) instead of a traditional cake. They're cheaper than most cakes and you won't have a cake cutting charge.

✳ **For the most dramatic savings,** create the cake yourself (or have a family member or friend do the honors).

✳ If you're hiring a baker, book early. There's only so much capacity a good baker will have, so make sure to get on his or her list as soon as you know your wedding date.

Opposite: A square cake allows for more slices. Left: Lavish "hat" cake designed and created by Dan Pasky. Some brides order a small, decorative cake to cut and then supplement it with cupcakes made with the same cake filling and icing as the embellished cake to reduce costs.

DIY LIGHTING

Lighting services can cost $2,000 and up per event, so if budget is a factor, can the wedding party do it themselves? Brian King, owner of BK the DJ (*bkthedj.com*), an event planning and lighting company in Washington, D.C., tells how:

USE UPLIGHTS. Rent Par 64 and Par 56 lights and bases (King used 12 lights at his reception). Create your plan so that there are outlets close to each fixture. Draw a diagram of the space, estimating where they'll work best. Spacing out these lights every 20 feet is a good rule of thumb.

REALIZE ARRANGING LIGHTS WILL BE TIME INTENSIVE. Enlist groomsmen or family friends to help set everything in place making sure they have a copy of the layout. The skill level you'll need? If someone is comfortable with wiring an audio system, they should be able to do this.

UPLIGHTS GET HOT. Position them so that guests, particularly children, won't interfere with them. Check with your venue regarding liability issues if you're setting up the lighting yourself. You'll need proper insurance.

NEW LIGHTING FIXTURES CAST OFF A BURNING ODOR WHEN YOU FIRST USE THEM. Turn on fixtures in a different location for an hour to eliminate the odor before the reception.

DEPENDING ON WHAT AND WHERE YOU'RE LIGHTING, a pure white beam of light may be too harsh. You can soften with colored gel filters chosen to match your color scheme. "I wouldn't recommend a couple set up their own gobo light to display initials and monograms during the reception," says King. "Couples can use PowerPoint with their initials in white over a black background and a projector instead."

Lights

Critical to the mood and tone you want to set, so much so that ugly-duckling venues can be transformed to look magical. Even if you're not familiar with event lighting lingo—for example, whether you'll need a pin-spot (focused light beam), gobos (the stencils placed over light sources to create patterns to be projected) or LEDs (light emitting diodes)—Brian Winthrop, president of Big Wave Event Productions (*bigwaveint.com*) in Roxbury, Connecticut, offers some advice:

❋ **The right lighting can save you big dollars** from having to transform a space with flowers and other decorations.

❋ **Use one color wash for the walls and another for the ceilings** for the most transformative effects. Magenta and amber washes are phenomenal for making guests, food and decor look great. It's been our experience that people dance and mingle less when we wash a room with blue light. They even seem to talk less, so I wouldn't recommend it for a wedding.

* **With "intelligent lighting"** (digitally controlled mutable lighting), you're able to project whatever patterns you want (a star field, slow-moving billowy clouds, the bride's and groom's initials) throughout the event space. You can also change the lighting at different times during the reception, for example, having one lighting palette for dinner and another for dancing.

* **Always light the dance floor properly.** When people dance at a wedding, it's a good sign that they're having a good time.

Reception music:
Making the price sound good

About 85% of couples choose DJs over live bands, and it's easy to see why: The cost of DJs averages between $100 and $300 per hour, and the average fee for bands (four hours, five musicians) runs between $3,000 and $5,000. Here are other ways to keep music costs within your budget:

* **Create your own iPod playlist** and rent the sound equipment. Your total outlay should be no more than several hundred dollars.

* **Choose different styles of music** for the cocktail reception/dinner and dancing. Have a playlist with at least four hours' worth of music for the cocktails/dinner and four or more for after-dinner dancing (and it never hurts to program more than you think you'll need).

* **Create separate playlists** for the special dances—bride and groom's first dance, mother and son dance, father and daughter dance, etc.

* **Mix fast with slow** so guests of different ages will find a reason to hit the dance floor. You probably don't need help in putting a playlist together, but if you do, go to *audiostiles.com*. They'll create customized lists of programmed music, from $50 per hour.

* **Get a close friend to play DJ**—oversee the playlist, monitor the audio equipment, the loudness of the music, etc.

* **If you book a DJ,** negotiate overtime rates upfront. It prevents costly surprises later!

* **If you opt for a DJ,** as with other vendors, you'll be able to negotiate discounts if you've chosen to marry during an off season, or on a less-in-demand day.

* **Use a playlist for the cocktail hour and reception,** and book a DJ or band for just the after-dinner dancing to stay within your budget.

Transportation

There's the old saying that in life it's all about the journey, not the destination, but on your wedding day, it is most definitely about the destination and getting there on time! Transportation costs run about 2% of a wedding budget, or about $500–$600, but can vary widely depending on the city and part of the country you're in.

BOOKING A LIMOUSINE

Pricing differs not only around the country (from $50 to $200 per hour for a limo, plus 15%–20% gratuity), but also among limo companies within an area. Most companies have a three-hour minimum. If you hold the ceremony and reception at the same site, you'll only have to rent a car to the site. One limo for the bride and her father (a car with enough room so gowns don't scrunch) may be all you need. Let the rest of the bridal party, the groom and his parents drive themselves.

* **Book a basic limo** without the TV, bar (stocked with Champagne) and other frills. You'll have plenty of other opportunities to toast your marriage. And are you really going to watch TV as you drive around on your wedding day?

* **Black limos** are generally less expensive to rent than white.

* **Rent a luxury sedan or town car rather than a limo.** It will be less costly.

* **Book your car or cars at least two months before the wedding;** three months in peak seasons.

* **Try to negotiate the minimum hours required,** particularly if you're doing a one-way trip. Or book a limo for what's called a "pickup and drop," and you'll just be paying for the individual ride.

* **If the company you work for uses a car service** you like, see if you can negotiate a discount.

* **Try to find the best limo service** nearest to where you'll be getting ready on the day of your wedding. As the meter starts running when the chauffeur pulls away from the rental lot, you'll save.

* **Ask about the size of the fleet.** If it's small (and they contract out for additional cars from other vendors), find out how they'll guarantee you'll get the exact car you want for your wedding day.

* **Do due diligence.** Insist on seeing the car. How new is it? What's the interior like? If you can, meet the driver. What will his attire be? What's his track record when it comes to being on time?

* **Find out how often the cars are cleaned and waxed.**

* **Get the overtime policy spelled out in detail.** The same for the tip—is the 15%–20% gratuity added to the final bill, or is a cash gratuity preferred (or expected)?

* **No detail is too small to have in writing:** the car model, condition, condition of the interior, driver's attire, cleanliness, promptness, etc. Specify exact pickup times and that you won't be paying overtime if the driver shows up an hour earlier than booked.

* **Have a detailed call sheet** if you're hiring a number of cars for your wedding. Regardless of the number, reconfirm a week before, then again several days or the day before the wedding.

OTHER COST-SAVING OPTIONS

* **Rent a luxury sedan from a car rental company** and have a friend or family member drive it to the ceremony, reception, airport, etc. (Someone willing to be the designated driver and forgo alcohol at the reception.)

* **Check in with antique and classic car groups** and associations to see if you can rent a fabulous vintage car. The fees could be quite reasonable.

affordable receptions

CHAPTER 7

ALTERNATIVE CEREMONY and RECEPTION SITES

If you're reeling from the price quote you've just received for a reception at a traditional wedding facility, get creative. While conventional party spaces have much to offer and may be the way you decide to go, the downside at some sites, besides cost, might be an event that comes across as too packaged and predictable. If a venue is very popular, your wedding may be just one of many scheduled on your big day (the "wedding factory" syndrome)—so much for exclusivity!

It may require some digging to come up with the right site: What once were considered imaginative options, like museums, historical mansions, vineyards and wineries, have become so popular that many aren't the bargains they once were. Still, there are well-priced options to unearth with a little research.

FINDING A UNIQUE WEDDING SITE

Weddingmapper.com has sites (and other wedding vendors) listed by city; user reviews. You can ask local brides/ couples for recommendations or their experiences with a site or vendor.

Eventective.com

Onewed.com

Uniquevenues.com

Wedalert.com

Message boards on Yahoo, Yelp

WHAT TO ASK, WHAT TO LOOK FOR WHEN CONSIDERING AN ALTERNATIVE SITE

Weight the advantages: Generally, lower costs; a wider variety of settings; often a more flexible time frame in which to use the facility. You'll be able to work with your own caterer (or choose from a list of approved ones) so that gives you more menu options, too.

And disadvantages: You'll have to be your own wedding planner, coordinating caterers, music, sometimes even table, chair and tableware rentals. (And there's the after-party cleanup to organize.) If you're opting for a botanical garden site or park, there's the weather factor, which means you'll need a rainproof backup plan.

✳ **Is it large enough for all the guests?** Party planners usually allot 4 to 6 square feet per person for a cocktail party; for a dinner using round tables, about 8 square feet per person.

✳ **Caterers: Can you bring your own?** Do you need to work from a pre-approved list? What are the license and insurance requirements? Can you provide your own liquor?

alternative ceremony and reception sites

* **Is the kitchen/food prep area large enough and sanitary?** Will your caterers need to bring extra equipment, even refrigerators? Ask to speak to caterers who've worked in the space to assess what's needed.

* **Electrical capacity:** This can be an issue in older, historic sites. Will you need to rent generators? Are all the outlets in working order? Is there enough power for a band's or DJ's equipment?

* **Air conditioning/heat:** Will there be enough for the amount of guests? Is the space known for an excess of either (freezing guests in summer and replicating a heat wave in the depths of winter)?

* **Stairways and elevators:** Easily accessible and large enough to avoid a crush or an elevator line? Does the site have handicap access? Enough (and pleasant) restrooms?

* **Access:** What spaces in the venue will you be able to use during the rental? Are there rooms in which to change? For taking photos? Will the caterers and the team setting up the decorations have ample time to do so before the reception? Will there be sufficient time after the party for the cleanup crew to finish? Will you have access to the site (if desired) for a pre-wedding photo shoot? Any restrictions on noise levels, alcohol?

* **Know what the venue's insurance policy covers** and whether you'll need extra insurance. Are there union rules to follow?

* **For outdoor sites, four key words:** *Have a backup plan.* And will the backup plan end up costing you more than you've budgeted? If you decide to have a tent in case the weather is bad, keep in mind this will run you from $300 to $9,000 and more depending on size, structure, and air-conditioning or heating needs. And the tent rental fee usually doesn't include tables and chairs. To find the cost of a tent rental in your area, go to *alltimefavorites.com.*

* **Permits:** For any public space, park or garden, make sure to apply for them well in advance of your date. Certain public sites can involve a lot of red tape.

* **Road access:** The long and winding bucolic road leading to an historical site that's a romantic dream spring, summer and fall might be an ice-clogged nightmare in winter, so plan accordingly.

* **Is it all worth it?** When you total up the site and rental fees and factor in the extra time and effort that you, or someone you designate or have to hire, will need to coordinate everything at an alternative venue, will you end up with real savings? "You may be better off paying a little more for an all-inclusive at a more traditional site," says Sarah Doheny of Sarah's Events and Bridal, a Pennsylvania-based event planning company. But then again, if the venue is everything you want for your wedding backdrop, it's easier to take on the extra work and rationalize the possibly minimal cost differential.

Preceding spread: A bride and groom entering their reception at the Seattle Art Museum. Opposite: Interior view of the Lyman Estate near Boston, an 18th-century Federal-style house.
Page 100: Rear view of the Lyman Estate. Page 101, top: Cocktail reception at the Seattle Olympic Sculpture Park; bottom: Wedding ceremony at the Seattle Art Museum.

Venue options

❋ Historical sites, mansions, and houses: The incomparable architecture and period interior design are hard to beat, which is why historical sites have become so popular for weddings. But with popularity comes increased rental costs. Search for sites (local historical societies, preservation groups) outside major cities and you may be able to come up with a good deal. For example, the exquisite 18th-century Lyman Estate, a short drive outside of Boston, has a weekday rental rate of $1,000 (*lymanestate.org*; 781-893-7232). At the Ernest Hemingway Home (*hemingwayhome.com*) in Key West, Florida, rentals begin at $1,500 in off-season.

❋ Bed-and-breakfasts have seen an uptick in weddings, an outgrowth of the interest in historical sites. At many B&Bs you can have your wedding cake (meaning the complete party setup an historical house might not offer) and eat it, too. But at the better-known and larger bed-and-breakfasts/inns, the cost per person can compete with a hotel's pricing. B&Bs outside popular vacation and resort areas are where the bargains are; for example, the $25-per-person wedding brunch at the Lilac Inn in Brandon, Vermont (near Middlebury), *lilacinn.com*. For a list of B&Bs that host weddings, go to *bnbfinder.com*.

alternative ceremony and reception sites

✳ **College clubs:** If your school doesn't have one in your immediate area, you can join as an out-of-town member and often access a network of reciprocal clubs throughout the U.S. The bigger-name clubs will have wedding packages that might run as much as a traditional wedding party site, but there are well-priced options, too, like the College Club of Boston (*thecollegeclubofboston. com*; 617-536-9510) with wedding packages starting at $1,250.

✳ **On-campus venues:** Even if you're not an alum (or part of the faculty or administration), reception rooms may be available to rent at a reasonable fee.

✳ **Museums/art galleries:** With the increase in the number of art museums and galleries over the last decade, there are more choices than ever. Check your local museum or gallery website; even if event facilities aren't listed, call to see if a particular gallery or space in the museum might be available for a party. The bigger museums in larger cities can command hefty price tags, and there are likely to be restrictions on hours of usage, depending on when the site is open to the public. But there are some extraordinary venues at less-than-extraordinary prices. For example, the Seattle Art Museum rents spaces for SAM Downtown, the Seattle Asian Art Museum or the Olympic Sculpture Park, starting at $500 (*seattleartmuseum.org/aboutus/faq/facilities.asp*). In New York City, one of the best-priced rental spaces is the BAM Café at the Brooklyn Academy of Music, starting at $1,500 (*bam.org*; 718-636-4198).

Above: The Miami Beach Botanical Garden.

✳ **Gardens/arboretums:** When flowers and trees are in bloom, what better backdrop? For public gardens, fees are low, usually under $100, but generally only wedding ceremonies (no receptions) are allowed. And since they are *public* gardens, you may have to contend with onlookers, or whatever else may be going on in the park on your wedding day. In New York's Central Park, a permit costs $25, unless you wed at The Conservatory Garden, which costs $400 (*centralparknyc.org*). In Atlanta, a favorite wedding site is the Atlanta Botanical Garden (*atlantabotanicalgarden.org*), where fees for ceremonies begin at $300 for the Japanese Garden and $600 for the Fragrance Garden. There are indoor facilities for receptions, too, at higher pricing. At the Miami Beach Botanical Garden (*mbgarden.org*), fees start at $500.

✳ **Municipal sites:** There are some architectural gems among the city halls, courthouses and libraries constructed in the early 20th century throughout the U.S. Many of these buildings rent out space for events, for example, the glorious Rotunda and Rotunda Gallery in Minneapolis (*www.municipalbuildingcommission. org*; 612-596-9518, charges from $1,000 to $1,700 depending on the day of the week).

alternative ceremony and reception sites

Left: The Commandant's House, dating from 1805, overlooks Boston Harbor.
Below: The Minneapolis City Hall & Hennepin County Courthouse.

✳ **Restaurants:** As convenient as traditional wedding reception venues, with menus that can be wider-ranging and diverse. Most important, the size of your party and the size of the restaurant need to mesh. If your guest list is large, will you be able to take over the entire restaurant for the duration of your reception? The owner will have to determine whether you're bringing him enough business to do so. If it's a dinner-only restaurant, consider scheduling a brunch or lunch. If the restaurant closes on a particular day each week, would that work for your wedding plans?

Other factors to consider: Will all your guests be in one room, or are tables spread out among several? Will there be room for live music if you want that?

If you're using a private reception room, does it have the same atmosphere as the restaurant? (Sometimes these rooms can be a bit sterile.) And how private is the room? Will you have to contend with other customers milling about should your reception be during a time when the restaurant is open?

* **Golf courses:** Luscious, verdant settings in season, and with a clubhouse close at hand, golf courses can be good choices for either outdoor or indoor weddings. "Your best deals will be on public courses outside major cities," says Sarah Doheny of Sarah's Events and Bridal. Venue costs can be reasonable, particularly on "off" nights at the club. For example, The Bridges Golf Club in San Ramon in the San Francisco Bay area has event rooms starting at $300, with entire clubhouse rentals beginning at $1,000 (*thebridgesgolf.com*; 925-735-4253 x102). The cons: You usually have to be a member of the club or have one sponsor you. Clubhouse decor can be very sporty, so it might take a lot of decorating to make a room look festive enough. Most likely, you'll have to work with the club caterer, so check out the food first.

* **Houses of worship:** Event spaces attached to a church or synagogue can be exceptionally well priced, plus there won't be any transportation costs to the reception site.

* **Tents:** Whether on the beach, in someone's backyard or in a garden, they'll protect against the elements, but you still have to heat them in winter and cool them in summer. "Going the tent route can be just as expensive as a traditional venue in some parts of the country," says Julia Erlichman of Philadelphia-based Julia & Friends Event Management (*juliaandfriends.com*). "Factor in the cost of the rental, the floor, heating or air conditioning, lighting, tables, chairs and tableware."

Opposite: The Bridges Golf Club in San Ramon, California.

BEACH WEDDINGS

Beaches have been a favorite low-cost site for years. Not only are the usage fees minimal, when the weather complies, the settings are incomparable. If you have your heart set on a beach wedding, here's what to keep in mind (for the tips below, we're referring to local beach weddings, rather than destination weddings taking place in a beach setting):

∗ Decide whether you'll go with the ceremony as well as the reception at the beach.

∗ First and foremost, check on the permit situation with the local or town municipality. Will you be able to set up a canopy or tent? Is there a limit to the number of people you can invite? Most public beaches don't allow alcohol, but is there a place nearby where you could set up a tent without such a restriction?

∗ Visit the beach at various times of day—how crowded is it, how near will beachgoers be to your intended site? How close will you be to the shoreline? (Remember, tides come in as well as go out.) Winds kick up as the sun goes down on many beaches—determine how that will impact what you plan.

∗ Even if a beach isn't typically windy, you never know what the weather may bring, so make plans to tie down items like programs, placecards and menus.

∗ Access: Is there a boardwalk or some sort of pathway? Or will your guests have to traipse over the sand, dodging Frisbee and volleyball games? If your caterer has to bring heavy equipment, how will he or she get it to the site? What are the bathroom facilities and how many cars can park nearby?

∗ Choose a caterer who has worked in a beach setting before. They'll be aware of things you'd never think of.

∗ Audio control: The surf (and seagulls!) might muffle your "I Do"s, so plan for a microphone that doesn't need an electrical outlet. Make sure whatever music group or entertainment you're hiring has the right generators and equipment for a beach locale.

∗ Go to *weather.com* for great tips for outdoor and beach weddings, such as using citronella candles to keep bugs away; adding tiny weights to your veil so that it won't lift in the breezes coming off the ocean; and avoiding metal folding chairs, which can turn hot as a car steering wheel when left to bake in the sun (opt for wooden chairs instead).

alternative ceremony and reception sites

CHAPTER 8

FLOWERS

Wedding flowers can enhance even the most glorious gown and add gorgeous and romantic touches to ceremony and reception decor. But floral beauty has its price—the average cost of wedding flowers runs about $1,820, according to *Brides.com*, and bouquets from $100–$500 depending on the survey.

With those numbers in mind, here are things to consider when planning your wedding flowers.

Below: Lily "clutch" bouquet.
Opposite: Mix favorite blooms
with inexpensive filler.

Bouquets

✳ **Keep it simple.** The more "arranged" and the more types of flowers that go into a bouquet, the more expensive it will be. Cascades, Biedermeiers, composites and pomander balls (for attendants and flower girls) are the most labor intensive for a florist, which you'll see reflected in their price. If you choose flowers that are delicate to handle, like gardenias and orchids, the price will reflect that, too.

✳ **Stay with in-season flowers.** As much as you love peonies, do you want to pay a premium to have them at your October wedding? A florist will help you with "replacement" options if your favorite buds are out of season. (*See peony substitutions on page 114.*)

✳ **Source flowers with wholesalers in your city and online.** When buying from a wholesaler, realize you may have to purchase larger quantities of a particular flower than you were planning. If you're not familiar with a wholesaler, see if they've been reviewed on *projectwedding.com* or *weddingwire.com*. You can also check out a vendor by inquiring on a wedding message board like *Yelp.com* or with the Better Business Bureau (*bbb.org*). Always know the guarantee and refund policy.

LOW-COST BOUQUET OPTIONS

✳ **The single-stem bouquet:** A perfect rose, peony or lily. (Jennifer Garner used a single calla for her bouquet when she married Ben Affleck.)

✳ **The arm bouquet:** Easily made with several long-stem flowers and filler.

✳ **Nosegays:** Small bouquets with just a few flowers and a lot of filler.

✳ **Ballerina:** A bouquet that uses tulle as filler and requires only a few flowers. Popular with brides during World War II. Has a vintage feel.

❋ **Mix silk and real flowers.**

❋ **Make a toss bouquet** using less expensive flowers in the same color scheme as your primary bouquet or make the toss in a ribbon and silk flower combination.

"ALTERNATIVE" BOUQUETS

❋ **Bridal muffs (winter):** In vintage fur, faux fur, velvet or other heavy fabric, with a floral spray attached.

❋ **Crystal bead bouquets:** Costly if purchased, but a relatively easy DIY project, which can be completed well in advance of a wedding. Easy instructions on *ehow.com* and *associatedcontent.com*.

❋ **Feather bouquets:** Ethereal concoctions often interwoven with ribbons and beading, pearls, crystals and rhinestones. For stylish examples, go to *emplume.com*.

INEXPENSIVE "CLUTCH" BOUQUETS

Hand-tied (also called "clutch") bouquets with stems wrapped simply and left exposed are the easiest type of bouquet to make. Here are suggestions from top event planners, florists and floral wholesalers for fabulous low-cost combinations you can put together yourself.

EMILY CANDEE, co-owner of Vine Floral & Event Design (*vinenyc.com*), based in New York

SPRING: Mix lilac and tulips with one or two peonies.

SUMMER: Make an all-hydrangea bouquet, using local hydrangea, or mix with roses and maybe a calla lily or two.

LATE SUMMER, EARLY FALL: Combine dahlias, celosia and viburnum berry.

WINTER: Amaryllis is a great winter flower, paired with some red ilex berry. Anemones are also available in winter and are stunning on their own or with some ranunculus or roses.

MARK HAYES, owner of *Flowerbud.com*
• Tie white irises (about 6–20) with raffia.
• Combine roses, tulips, and calla lilies (8 of each flower) with salal filler* (its deep green leaves work well in bouquets).
• Mix roses and freesia, 12 of each flower, with salal filler.
• Combine roses, hypericum, and parrot tulips (6 roses, 12 parrots, 5 hypericum), no filler.

*We also recommend that brides, or whoever among friends and family is preparing the bouquet, head outside and cut some greens from their garden to use as filler.

From **SANDRA PINEDA,** owner of *WholeBlossoms.com*, a Texas-based flower company
• Mix spider mums with roses.
• In season, add hydrangea to the spider mums and spray roses.
• Blend roses and gerberas.

"Simply wrap white tulips in thick white ribbon," says **JULIA ERLICHMAN** of Julia & Friends Event Management.

SEASONAL FLOWER GUIDE*

YEAR-ROUND FLOWERS: Carnations, delphinium, lilies, orchids, roses, ranunculus, stephanotis

SPRING: Anemone, freesia, daffodils, iris, peonies, tulips

SUMMER: Asters, azalea, gardenia, hydrangea, iris, lily of the valley, peonies, snapdragon

FALL: Hydrangea, jasmine, sunflowers

WINTER: Amaryllis, freesia, gentian roses, poinsettia

* The California Cut Flower Commission site, *ccfc.org*, is a wonderful resource with a detailed in-season flower guide and color chart. There are flower trend reports and bouquet and centerpiece ideas, too. Also check out *theflowerexpert.com*, a flower encyclopedia, and *fiftyflowers. com*. For a general flower guide, go to *sierraflowerfinder.com*, a professional florist's reference for over 2,500 different types of flowers.

DIY wedding bouquets

HAND-TIED ROSE WEDDING BOUQUET

from Save-on-crafts.com

MATERIALS

2 dozen spray of baby's breath, gypsophila or lilies of the valley
24 small roses
12 large roses
12 medium roses in complementary or contrasting color
3 yards white satin ribbon
ivy garland, vine or branches
clippers or scissors
floral wire or raffia
pearl-topped corsage pins

Make the morning of the wedding. Keep flowers in water until the last possible moment.

1. Clean rose stems, removing lower greenery, extra or untidy or unattractive leaves, and thorns.

2. Cut flowers 2" from bottom at an angle. Best to do this while the stems are still under water and allow them a few seconds to further hydrate.

3. Create individual stems from the baby's breath. Cut the ivy into sections of 8"–12" each.

4. Add a stem of baby's breath to 2 rose stems. Holding the stems upright in your hand, gradually add more stems to the bouquet at a 45-degree angle, turning the bouquet in your hand so that a spiral gradually develops. Hold the stems firmly at the binding point while slowly adding more flowers.

5. Insert greenery (ivy, leafed branches) throughout the bouquet. Greenery brings out the flowers if placed carefully and sparingly around each bloom.

6. Once you are happy with the overall size, shape and color of the bouquet, tie the stems together at the top and bottom. Tie flowers with a tight rubber band or floral wire about 4" below flower heads (or middle of stem) and at end of stem. Wrap securely. Then, with sharp scissors or pruners, trim the stems at the bottom so that they are all the same length.

7. Use the satin ribbon to tightly wrap the stems. Start at the base of the flowers (the top of the bouquet), leaving enough ribbon to tie a knot later (about 3"). Overlap each twist to conceal the wire and the stems, working from top to bottom. When you reach the bottom, tuck the ribbon over the base of the stems and then wind the ribbon back up the stems (use a corsage pin to hold ribbon in place on the bottom—remove later). When you reach the starting point, tie the ribbon in a knot (with the beginning of the ribbon). Push the knot into the top of the ribbon to conceal it. Use 3 pearl-topped corsage pins to fasten the ribbon securely to the stems. Be sure to push the pins at a slant downward into the stems. This will also give the bouquet a finished look.

8. Set bouquet in an empty vase that has a narrow opening until ready to use. Wrap in tissue paper and store in the fridge.

Above: Rose, spray rose, and ranunculus bouquet, Vine Floral & Event Design.

LEAST EXPENSIVE FLOWERS
Alstroemeria, carnations, freesia, daisies, hydrangea, mums

MOST EXPENSIVE FLOWERS
"Calla lilies, phalaenopsis orchids/ cymbidium orchids (most orchids in general), Dutch hydrangea and peonies. Lily of the valley and sweet peas are also pricey," says Emily Candee of New York's Vine Floral & Event Design.

LESS-EXPENSIVE PEONY SUBSTITUTES Want the peony look without the cost? Sandra Pineda of *WholeBlossoms.com* recommends the following garden roses: Agnes Schilliger, Althea, Antique Romantica, Baby Romantica, Baby Candy Romantica, Carmeline, Mistinguett.

ANOTHER FLORIST FAVORITE FOR A PEONY SUBSTITUTE the David Austin Peony Rose Pink Phoebe.

SPRINGTIME IN ENGLAND BOUQUET
designed by Chelsea Fuss for OnceWed.com

MATERIALS
10 red/white anemone stems
3 full pink roses
10 ranunculus stems in eggplant
2 bunches of buttercup greens
2 bunches of vinca vine
2 stems of green hellebores
clippers or scissors
twine
ribbon (1.5 yards)
pins

1. Remove most of the leaves from anemone and ranunculus stems.

2. Place a small group of flowers in your hand. Add roses at the bottom and let the ranunculus buds peek out at the top. Turn the bouquet each time you add a new grouping of flowers. Keep turning and adding flowers until you are pleased with the composition. Place greens around the bottom of the bouquet.

3. Secure with twine.

4. Clip the stems so they are all the same length.

5. Wrap ribbon around stem and secure with two pins.

For boutonnières, work with the same flowers or colors used for the bride and bridesmaid bouquets. With boutonnières, a flower and stem should be about 3" in length. Tuck a bit of greenery and baby's breath behind the flower. Baby's breath goes in the middle and greenery should be slightly visible at the side of the flower, but not too much above it. Wrap stems with wire and cover with floral tape. Fasten with a pin. Tuck in a little personal memento.

Flowers for the ceremony and reception site

(See Chapter 6 for reception decorating without flowers.)

❋ **Head to the supermarket.** "Go to Whole Foods, The Home Depot, or a supermarket and buy pots of daffodils, lilacs or orchids to use as centerpieces. These can become party favors, one for each table. Hire a college student, a friend's son or daughter, to paint or wrap the pots to go with your reception color scheme and then to set everything up on the wedding day," says Julia Erlichman of Julia & Friends Event Management.

✳ **Make a deal at the local farmers' market.** "If you're going to need a particular flower in quantity, befriend a supplier at your local farmers' market, which is what I did when I had to create 50 centerpieces for a summer wedding," says Erlichman. "I told them what I needed, chose zinnias as the flower, and was able to purchase them for $7 a bunch. I highly recommend zinnias for summer weddings. They're sturdy flowers with wonderful color."

✳ **Allot your flower budget to where it will have the most impact.** "Spend the money where you'll see it," says Emily Candee of Vine Floral & Event Design. "A ceremony might only be 20 minutes, while the reception is four hours, so plan your flower budget accordingly."

✳ **Alternate flowers and candles.** "Use floral arrangements on half the reception tables; candles and floating flower head tablescapes on the others," says Candee.

✳ **Look at inexpensive, untraditional fillers.** Use fruit (pears, apple, lime) in table flower arrangements to help fill them out and save money.

✳ **Or make filler the main attraction.** Go with just flower filler, e.g., ivy, baby's breath, Queen Anne's lace, for your centerpieces.

✳ **Think big.** "For any church or large area that needs a good-sized bouquet just to be seen, choose impactful flowers like hydrangeas and football mums," says Chris O'Dowd of The Cantering Caterer. "The larger the flower, the fewer you'll need. And hydrangeas can make the most wonderful, simple-to-assemble, inexpensive centerpieces: All you need is a bunch or two and a glass bowl."

✳ **Go super-modern** "so that it looks as if you're making a style rather than budget statement," says Emily Candee. "Buy tall cylinder vases, fill with large leaves (philodendron, monstera, sago or areca palm leaves) and/or steel grass. The centerpieces can be worked to look minimalist and sculptural."

❧ SOURCES

FIFTYFLOWERS.COM Wide range of flowers, DIY wedding combos, seasonal flower guide.

FLOWERBUD.COM Everything from Asiatic lilies to peonies, bouquets.

THEFLOWEREXCHANGE.COM Range of flowers, wedding blog and floral supplies.

WHOLEBLOSSOMS.COM Wide flower selection, bouquets, DIY flower blog, care tips.

* **Mix expensive flowers with inexpensive ones** to stretch your dollar. For example, mix one peony with lots of roses and ranuncula for each centerpiece, says Beth Helmstetter of Beth Helmstetter Events.

* **Let your flowers glow.** Add dazzle to your tablescapes by placing submersible Floralytes in the clear vases holding your flowers.

* **Rent the flowers and greenery.** See if you can rent potted plants from a nursery to use at the ceremony or reception site.

* **If you're decorating with rose petals,** order freeze-dried petals online. They're much cheaper than fresh and look good.

Should you do your own wedding flowers?

You can save a bundle, but there's work involved for you or your family and friends. Here's what Mark Hayes of *Flowerbud.com* recommends:

* **Arrangements should be uncomplicated,** with readily available and easy-to-find (and easy-to-work-with) flowers.

* **Work with fairly sturdy flowers,** like roses or any of the bulb flowers.

* **Arranging flowers takes time.** Do you want to be doing this right before your ceremony? Maybe not. Do you have a team of family and friends that will have the time to assemble the arrangements without feeling frantic or rushed?

* **Have a test run.** Order a small sample of the flowers you'd like to use for your wedding from the supplier you've chosen. See what's involved in assembling a small centerpiece or bouquet that's close to what you'll want on your wedding day.

* **When working with lilies,** clip the stamen so that none of the pollen spills to your dress (if they are used for a bouquet) or table linens (if part of a centerpiece).

* **If you're envisioning big arrangements,** or want to work with out-of-season flowers, it's probably best to enlist a florist.

Opposite: Tablescape alternating candles and flowers at the Olympic Sculpture Park in Seattle.

Ordering flowers online

* **Timing their arrival:** "As most flowers are shipped in bud form, arrange to have them 2 to 3 days before the wedding," says Hayes. Lilies should arrive earlier as they can take 5 to 7 days to open. Check with your supplier and plan accordingly.

* **When flowers arrive,** someone should be at home to receive them.

* **Flowers will wilt if left too long** in direct sunlight or extreme hot or cold temperatures. As soon as possible after you receive the flowers, cut the stems and place them in water.

* **To have on hand before flowers arrive:** Several 5-gallon buckets, fresh water, flower food, pruning shears, and for roses, a rose stripper to remove excess leaves and thorns.

* **Storing the flowers:** Best in a room between 65°F and 72°F, free of drafts and not in direct sunlight, or near heat vents, recommends Hayes. Flowers don't have to be refrigerated. If kept too cold, flowers will remain closed.

flowers

CHAPTER 9

The BIG PICTURE

Most wedding planners will tell you that photography is probably not the best area in which to cut corners. Photographers, of course, will tell you this, too! The reasoning is pretty fail-proof: Once-in-a-lifetime moments are just that, and who wants a blurry photo as you exchange your first just-married kiss, or worse, no photo documentation of it at all?

Photography averages 7% to 10% (some estimates go as high as 15%) of an overall wedding budget, with beginning packages starting at $1,000, an entire day's booking at about $3,000. For full coverage, expect a photographer to shoot about 2,000 pictures, from which he or she selects the 400 to 500 you then choose from. Whatever you decide to spend, here's how to maximize your precious photo dollars.

If money is tight

Hire a photographer for the ceremony only and have friends and family document the reception.

If you can stretch the budget a bit more, go for a "shoot and burn" package, says Tracey Brown of Tracey Brown Photography (*traceybrownphoto.com*) in Atlanta. With a "shoot and burn," you generally get a photographer for four hours, and then all the unedited, minimally retouched, high-resolution images on a DVD.

* **"Prioritize what you must have covered,"** says Brown. "Be aware when you book a minimum fixed-hour package that weddings often run behind schedule, so decide what's important to you: the wedding preparation and ceremony? The ceremony and opening moments of the reception or cocktail party?"

* **Head to a nearby, smaller community to look for photography and video talent,** if you live in a major city where the cost of wedding photography is high.

* **Like a studio's style? Hire one of their lesser-known or junior photographers** (checking work and references, of course) rather than an expensive "name" shooter.

* **Whatever the experience level, make sure the person you're hiring is the one who will turn up the day of the wedding,** not an assistant or someone you haven't met with.

* **Do you feel comfortable going with really new talent?** Look at the portfolios of photographers in fine arts and photography masters programs at nearby colleges and universities. Give the person a small assignment first to see how he or she works and whether the results are what you expected.

* **Two are better than one.** If you absolutely can't afford a professional photographer and are thinking of enlisting a friend or family member to document your wedding, double up. Top studios often send a "second shooter" on wedding assignments to make sure their team captures every key moment. By having two amateurs rather than one, you're increasing the odds for getting good coverage on your wedding day.

* **Find out how a photographer works.** Once you've reviewed a portfolio, check references for punctuality and work style (slow, fast, unobtrusive). Specify attire—you don't want an overdressed photographer sweltering at a ceremony or reception that might take place outdoors if the weather is good; nor do you need someone resembling a surfer dude snapping away at the main altar in the local cathedral.

* **Your guests as paparazzi:** Whether you're on a tight budget or not, it's fun to include disposable cameras at each guest table for candid shots.

* **Tailor the package.** Studio packages outline what you get for each level of pricing. Negotiate not only the price but also what the package includes. Maybe you don't want formal portrait shots; see if you can have an extra hour of reception coverage instead.

* **Ask about your photographer's backup plans in case of illness or other emergency.** Are there colleagues who will step in to take the place of the person you hired? Find out who that might be and look at his or her work.

* **Buy photo rights for unlimited personal usage.** Check your contract carefully so that there are no restrictions on the time frame for making prints or number of copies made per image. This way you can reprint from your disc whenever you like. (Photo developers will ask to see the copyright/permissions status before printing a photographer's work.) Get the rights to post on your website/blog/social networking site, too.

* **Inquire about retouching costs:** Basic retouching for color and lighting is included in most packages; more extensive adjustments bring extra fees, so have everything clarified and in writing. (For do-it-yourself retouching, a free site is *Picnik.com*.)

* **If you have a friend who's a good photographer, book a "day-after" session** (this can be his or her wedding gift to you). Assuming you're not departing immediately for your honeymoon, a "day-after" shoot (with the couple attired in wedding clothes) allows for more relaxed images, as well as the so-called "trash the dress" session, where the bride is photographed walking in her gown at water's edge, through the dunes, sitting on the ballroom floor. (And the dress doesn't really have to get "trashed"; it just receives more of a workout.)

- You should really want to work with the photographer, really love his or her pictures. I ask potential clients if they'd like to meet over dinner, so I can better understand what they're looking for and we can get to know one another in a relaxed setting. It's preferable to just coming to the studio to look at a portfolio.

- When reviewing a prospective photographer's work, you should have an emotional response to the images.

- Use a professional makeup artist? If you can afford one, it helps the final quality of the pictures. But you should look like yourself and not go overboard with makeup. What I want to photograph is you.

- If you have to prioritize within your photo budget, forgo the albums; you can do them later. But don't cut down on coverage time. Some of the sweetest moments occur as the bride and groom are getting ready, so you want to be able to allow for that.

- If you can only book a photographer for a few hours, eliminate the reception shoot. It's better to have those getting-ready pix. Enlist friends and family to take care of the reception.

- Don't expect your photographer to wing it and get all of the pictures you need. I ask for a timeline, as well as a list of the family and guests that must be covered in addition to the bridal party. This way no one forgets Grandpa. But I also recommend not going overboard with family pictures. No more than 20, or the couple gets short shrift. And if everyone's tied up having their pictures taken, there's a huge lag in time between the ceremony and reception when the bride and groom and their families aren't mingling with guests.

- Don't sweat it when the weather isn't good. A cloud-covered sky affords the perfect light for portraits—no shadows or harshness. If it rains, shots with umbrellas can be fun.

Find your photographer

We asked Connie Miller of Studio Atticus (*studioatticus.com*) in Boston and Meg Perotti (*megperotti.com*) in Los Angeles, both known for their evocative wedding photography, for advice on how to choose a photographer. Connie Miller's recommendations:

✳ **Really critique the work.** Ask to see samples of different weddings they've photographed—casual, formal, winter, summer, on the beach.

✳ **Review at least 100 shots from a particular wedding.** You may love the photographer's work, but if his or her style is photojournalistic and you were seeking more of a fine-art touch, will you be happy with the final results?

✳ **As you look at the pictures,** was the photographer "in the moment," capturing not only the key events, but the mood, emotions and spontaneous happenings that make for the most memorable photographs?

✳ **The photographer is an integral part of your event;** ask yourself, is this someone you and your family and guests will enjoy having around?

Maximizing your photographer's time

✳ **Check the religious site's policy on photography.** Is anything off limits; are there any restrictions to photographing during the actual ceremony? You don't want to have to pay a photographer to sit there like a guest.

✳ **Do portraits right before the ceremony.** "I know it's tradition and often the bride and groom don't want to see each other before the wedding, but if they're paying a hefty day or half-day rate, I recommend getting the portraits out of the way before the ceremony," says Miller. "It's efficient and the photos are taken while the couple is fresh. Then the bride and groom can mingle with their guests during the cocktail hour, usually the time these pictures are taken, and enjoy themselves."

✳ **"Limit the portraits,"** says Miller. "They can become very time-consuming when you try to please all your relatives and friends. You just need six shots: the bride and groom, the couple with his family, with her family, the bride with her bridesmaids, the groom with the groomsmen and the couple with their entire wedding party. That's it."

✳ **Create a "photo booth"** for your guests. Lighting, a backdrop, maybe a chair, and a camera on a tripod with a self-timer are all that is required. Guests take their own pictures, freeing up the photographer to wander about and record those spontaneous and capture-the-moment shots.

Destination beach wedding photography

Chris Mann, photographer at of Tropical Imaging Turks and Caicos (*tropicalimaging.com*), a photography studio based in Providenciales, Turks and Caicos, provides some detailed advice.

✳ **Know your beach.** Before you finalize plans, find out as much as you can about a beach's location: the direction it faces, the sand composition, likely traffic and what surrounds it. A beach that is sunlit in the afternoon in January may be shaded in June.

　◆ **Seek out a secluded or relatively secluded beach.** The beach nearest your hotel might not be the best option (too many well-wishing but nosy passersby).

　◆ **Check out, or have someone report back to you about, the beach's sand quality.** Some Caribbean islands have beaches made of a black volcanic grit rather than soft white sand.

　◆ **After high tide, does the beach accumulate seaweed** or any other flotsam? If so, make plans to have the beach swept and raked before your wedding.

　◆ **Which direction does the beach face?** Before you select your ceremony site, make sure you won't have to look directly into the sun as it sets, otherwise there'll be a lot of squinting as you exchange your "I Do"s.

　◆ **When's high tide?** No need to have your guests sitting unexpectedly in ankle-deep water.

✳ **If the sun doesn't set over the ocean,** the effective sunset time will be up to half an hour earlier.

✳ **Take note of whether and when the sun slips behind your hotel** or other nearby buildings, even a cluster of trees, once it begins to set, and determine how that will impact the light at your beachside ceremony.

✳ **Know the exact sunset time.** The most popular time of day for a beach wedding is about an hour before sunset—the light is wonderful and the temperature is more comfortable than earlier in the day.

✳ **Don't start your ceremony at sunset**—any delays in actual start time might have you exchanging vows in the dark. Sometimes Jewish couples will opt for a sunset start time in accordance with their faith, but they usually arrange for portrait photos to be taken before the ceremony, or on another day.

* **Sunrise weddings can be quite nice,** for the same reasons that sunset ceremonies are—spectacular settings, comfortable temperatures—but few couples are keen on getting up at the crack of dawn to go through with them.

* **Clothing:** We've had grooms and groomsmen on tropical beaches who've rented morning suits with top hat and gloves, and as a result they've fried! If you want to wear a suit, it should be lightweight and made of natural fibers. Many grooms opt for khaki or white linen pants and a loose, open-neck shirt. For the bride a long train is not very practical on a beach. And the same advice applies as for the groom and his party—lightweight, natural fibers are the only way to go.

A wedding on Fryes Beach in Antigua.

Videography; digital and print albums

✱ **Skip the videography if you're looking to save money.** Family or friends can shoot if you need to have a moving-image record of your wedding day. Just as with stills, double up and have two amateurs, rather than one, film your event.

✱ **If you must have professional video, hire a videographer to shoot "straight" or "raw" footage only.** You can save on fees by editing the film yourself. (Even if you hire a videographer to film edit, ask for the raw footage anyway. Why not have every moment that was captured for your film archive?)

✱ **For do-it-yourself film editors:** Pinnacle Studio software, (*pinnaclesys.com*, from $49.99) helps the amateur film editor go for special effects, Hollywood style. For other options: TopTenREVIEWS ranked Cyberlink PowerDirector, Corel VideoStudio and Adobe Premiere Elements the top three video editing software programs (*video-editing-software-review.toptenreviews.com*). For reviews of free online editing sites, visit *extremetech.com*; for write-ups on free video editors, go to *pcmag.com*. (Prior to purchasing video editing software, check system requirements carefully.)

✱ **Create a digital wedding album rather than a print one** (that can come later). Such software as Wedding-Album-Maker (*Wedding-Album-Maker. com* from $29.95), or Wedding Slideshow Studio 1.01 (from $79.95) will help you make the most of your photo presentation, whether it's with jazzy transitions or pan-and-zoom effects. You can add background music, too. Remember, when contracting with a photographer, always buy the rights to copy, print or upload your wedding photos. It will keep costs down when creating an electronic or paper album.

✱ **Publish your own wedding album/book.** Sites like *MyPublisher.com* will help you create a wedding book at a reasonable price. Their 11.5" x 15" hardcover books with 20 pages of pictures printed coffee-table style (with 200 layout options) start at $59.80. At *blurb.com*, a large 13" x 11" hardcover book with photo-image wrap and 401–440 pages is $169.95. At *picaboo.com*, the design software (with 240 page layouts) is free. You can post the album online for free, or develop it in book format. 8.5" x 11" books start at $29.99 for 20 pages.

✱ **Supplement any digital or hardcover photo albums with a canvas "gallery wrap"** of favorite wedding images. With a gallery wrap, a picture is enlarged, printed on canvas, then wrapped, like a piece of art, around a wooden frame. At *updone.com*, the price for a 36" x 48" gallery wrap is $167. 40, less if you assemble the canvas yourself.

CHAPTER 10

HONEYMOONS

The average cost of a honeymoon in 2008 was $3,805, according to The Wedding Report. While the recent economic downtown may shrink that number in coming months, couples are not forgoing their honeymoon plans. "Budgets might be cut, the numbers of vacation days reduced, but the bride and groom still want to travel," says Peggy Knipp of Honeymoons Galore, a Nashville-based travel agency, where she plans about 150 to 200 honeymoon trips a year.

Make the most of your honeymoon dollars

HONEYMOON REGISTRIES

When someone says "china," do you dream of Shanghai rather than Lenox or Rosenthal? Prefer a hotel booking to an espresso maker? If that's the case, establish a honeymoon registry. It's similar to a traditional registry, but allows family and friends to gift parts of your honeymoon travel. Honeymoon registries have caught on as many couples, particularly if they've been living together or are marrying for a second time, have set up households and don't need tableware, appliances and the other practical items that are typical shower or wedding gifts.

Preceding spread: A white sand beach at Rum Point, on the North Coast of Grand Cayman. Below: Snorkeling off St. Thomas, in the U.S. Virgin Islands.

While many major travel companies—cruise lines, hotels, resorts, even certain destinations—offer registry services, the independent registries will offer the most flexibility. If you decide to open a honeymoon registry:

* **Create a detailed travel itinerary.** The sooner you write your wish list, the better. You and the registry service then break the trip into components, so that family and friends can contribute to specific aspects of your trip, for example, one night's accommodations, or dinner at a well-known restaurant at your destination. List desired activities, too: whether it's surfing lessons in Maui, a round of golf in the Bahamas, or theater tickets in New York or London.

* **Check the site's affiliations.** Some independent sites work with a particular travel agency and incentivize you to book your honeymoon with it. Look closely at the agency's pricing and find out what deals and discounts they can offer before signing on.

* **Carefully read the fine print on fees.** Registries will charge a service fee, generally from 7% to 9% (although it can range as high as 15%), payable by either the registered couple or their guests (or sometimes split between both). Fees cover the site's hosting features, such as the actual registry management and phone and e-mail support. Some fees are waived when a certain dollar amount of travel is booked through an affiliated travel partner. (*See above.*)

* **Popular travel registries include:** *travelersjoy.com. honeyluna.com, thebigday.com, honeymoonwishes.com, sendusoff.com.*

GO ON A CRUISE

The all-inclusive pricing makes it easier to budget, and with judicial planning, keep costs in check. And a cruise is often cheaper than a land-based trip. For example, a three- to four-night cruise with airfare will generally start at $1,600 per couple; $2,800 for seven nights, according to Bambi Duvall, owner of Virginia-based All About Travel (*allabouttravelblog.com*). Compare that to the average cost of seven nights with airfare in Hawaii ($7,000) and Europe ($6,000). For discounted cruises, see what your travel agent can come up with or find your own discounted cruise at *cruisedeals.com* and *cruisesonly.com.*

LOOK INTO ALL-INCLUSIVES

As with cruises, all-inclusive resorts offer a package that covers most of your expenses. "They're a big trend this year for couples looking to watch their budget," says Honeymoon Galore's Peggy Knipp. All-inclusive chains like Sandals (*sandals. com*), Occidental Hotels & Resorts (*occidentalhotels.com*), SuperClubs (*superclubs. com*) have long served the honeymoon crowd. For more ideas on all-inclusives, go to *allinclusiveoutlet.com, classicvacations.com*; for the Caribbean, Mexico and Hawaii. *honeymoonsinc.com.*

FOR DISCOUNTS ON TRAVEL

Of course you know about Expedia, Orbitz, CheapTickets and Hotels.com for getting low-priced deals on airfare and hotels. Expand your research to sites like *AllLuxuryHotels.com* for the best rates at four- and five-star properties around the world. For procrastinators or those fond of a certain serendipity to their holidays, *LastMinuteTravel.com* will unearth the best deals when you want to travel at very short notice. With many offers, you won't see the hotel name, but you can often figure that out from the property description. Search *Quikbook.com* for reduced hotel fares.

OFF-SEASON TRAVEL

As with non-honeymoon vacations, you'll get the most for your money if you travel during off or shoulder seasons. Keep in mind:

The "love bridge" at the Rockhouse Hotel, Negril, Jamaica.

* **The pros and cons of tropical destinations:** Those luscious five-star resorts at half price! That's what you'll find from May through September (and possibly through the week before Christmas depending on the hotel or resort) in top spots in Florida, Mexico and the Caribbean. But off-season prices come with a risk of hurricanes, steamy humidity and torrential afternoon thunderstorms.

* **Hurricane season** officially runs from June 1 to November 30 according to the National Oceanic and Atmospheric Administration. Ninety-six percent of major hurricanes hit between August and September, with maximum activity falling the first two weeks in September. Facts to consider: Hurricanes have formed in the Atlantic basin as early as March (in 1908) and as late as December (1954). For more information, go to *www.aoml.noaa.gov.*

* **There's much lower storm risk** if you stay below the hurricane belt. The Caribbean islands least likely to be hit by hurricanes are the ABC's of the Dutch Leewards: Aruba, Bonaire and Curaçao; the Windward Islands of Trinidad and Tobago; and Margarita Island, off the coast of Venezuela. Worth noting: Abaco and Grand Bahama in the Bahamas have seen the most hurricane activity since records have been kept. For an island-by-island breakdown of hurricane hits, go to *stormcarib.com* and *hurricanecity.com.*

* **Travel insurance and what it can and can't do for you:** There are a lot of "ifs, ands, or buts" with these policies. You'll have the best chance for reimbursement if your airline and hotel shuts down due to a hurricane before you start your travels. If you decide not to risk the trip, but the airport and hotel were open on your scheduled departure day, you might not be reimbursed. And once you are at a resort, it's much tougher to recoup vacation costs, even if your honeymoon is a complete washout. No matter what discounted rate you booked, being stuck in a hotel behind shuttered windows, with winds howling and rains pummeling the grounds, just isn't a bargain!

GAMING THE ODDS FOR GOOD WEATHER IN THE SHOULDER- AND OFF-SEASON TROPICS

Jen Carfagno, cohost of "First Outlook" on the Weather Channel (*weather.com*) and their Wedding Weather expert, tells you what you need to know.

When you're least likely to need an umbrella off season:

FLORIDA: April, May and October, November

JAMAICA, PUERTO RICO, ST. THOMAS: March, April and November

THE BAHAMAS: March through May

GRAND CAYMANS: May, June

CANCUN, MEXICO: May, June

HAWAII: May and June. Rainy season typically runs from November to February, which coincides with the islands' peak travel time. The rain doesn't last long, generally occurring overnight and early morning. Hurricanes are rare in Hawaii.

DRIEST AND LEAST HUMID CARIBBEAN ISLANDS: The ABC's—Aruba, Bonaire and Curaçao. And while historically they're the islands least likely to be hit by a hurricane, they're not completely immune, either.

READING INTO A FORECAST (or how to predict when sunny Florida won't be so sunny). The forecast calls for two weeks of partly cloudy/partly sunny weather with a 50% chance of rain. What's really in store—will you have an afternoon lying on the beach or will you have to run for cover? "Watch when the sea breezes are onshore," says Carfagno. "The resulting cooler air forms a boundary which precipitates rain storms. Check the Weather Channel's hour-by-hour forecasts—these have greatly improved in the last several years—and plan accordingly."

WHEN TO CANCEL THE TRIP: "I would say with a hurricane watch. Those are issued 36 hours in advance of a hurricane. When a hurricane or tropical storm threatens, it will likely be tracked on one of the maps featured on the *Weather.com* homepage. Check our projected path forecasts (sometimes called forecast swath) with the potential areas of impact."

* **Consider a city honeymoon.** You'll get great deals at top hotels in major U.S. cities like New York, Boston and Chicago in January, February and March (excluding Valentine's Day, and Easter and Passover, if they fall in March). There are very attractive summer rates on weekends in major, business-oriented cities, too, which can bring down your average cost per night, should you stay beyond Sunday. In warm weather, book a hotel with an outdoor pool, like the Colonnade in Boston, the Joule Hotel in Dallas, the Churchill Hotel in Washington, D.C., or the Four Seasons Hotel in Houston to give a resort-like feel to your city stay.

* **Head to a ski resort in summer.** A top-notch resort like Four Seasons Whistler can offer very attractive summer rates. And the ski and snowboard season lasts through August. Their recent "Stay Longer" package (one night free) averaged approximately $150 per night.

* **Spread the good news:** When booking your honeymoon, whether through a travel agent or directly with an airline or hotel, tell them you'll be on your honeymoon and ask if they have any special rates they can offer.

* **Let history be your guide:** If you're heading to tropical or warm-weather climates, make sure to research the weather history for your destination on the Weather Channel's wedding planner (*weather.com*). Register to see what the weather history has been for your destination—they'll break it down hour-by-hour for the last three years. (A must if you're planning an outdoor destination wedding.)

* **Book very early or very late** (see *lastminutetravel.com*) for the best deals.

* **Comparison shop within a hotel chain.** If you want the luxe experience offered by top hotel groups like the Ritz-Carlton, Mandarin Oriental or Four Seasons, compare rates among hotels within the region you'd like to go. While prices vary from one off season to the next (as well as with the state of the economy), consider the differences in recent off-season room rates at three Florida Ritz-Carltons: $143 at the Naples Golf Resort; $169 a night at Coconut Grove; and $219 at the Key Biscayne locale.

* **How to do Hawaii:** The Aloha State has long been a favorite honeymoon destination—and often an expensive one. Bambi Duvall, of All About Travel, says you can maximize your Hawaiian honeymoon dollars if you:
  * BOOK A CONDO RATHER THAN STAY AT A HOTEL. "There is a wide range in inventory, from budget to high-end," says Duvall. "Consult a travel specialist who is familiar with the properties. Online booking may not tell the true condition of the condo you're hoping to rent."
  * RENT A COMPACT CAR RATHER THAN A CONVERTIBLE.
  * STICK TO ONE ISLAND—save the island hopping for a later trip.

- **GO TO OAHU**—it prices out the best of all the islands and has a lot to offer: island history and tradition, and big surf on the north side.
- **EAT OUT FOR ONLY ONE MEAL A DAY**—and make that lunch for the best cost savings.

✳ **Pick good-value tropical isles,** says Peggy Knipp of Honeymoons Galore (*honeymoonsgalore.com*).
- **BEST-VALUE CARIBBEAN:** Aruba, Puerto Rico, St. Martin, St. Thomas
- **MOST EXPENSIVE ISLANDS:** Anguilla, Barbados, St. Bart's
- **MID-RANGE:** Antigua, St. Lucia
- **HAWAII:** "I'm a fan of Maui, and you can do it reasonably if you go with a condo. I recommend Condominium Rentals Hawaii (*crhmaui.com*) to get a sense of prices and packages there."

A private dip pool at Cocobay, an all-inclusive resort in Antigua, located on the sunset side of the island.

The swimming pool at El San Juan Hotel & Casino in Puerto Rico.

✳ Or try to find an attractive hotel rate on an expensive island.
We asked Liliane Nash, president of Humbert Travel (*humbertravel. com*), a division of Altour International, and a honeymoon specialist, for recommendations for good deals on some of the Caribbean's most expensive islands. Keep in mind, she says, if you are traveling in peak winter months, you'll get better rates in January than in February or March.

- **ANGUILLA:** CuisinArt
- **ANTIGUA:** Galley Bay Resort and Carlisle Bay
- **BARBADOS:** The Sandpiper Hotel, Colony Club
- **ST. BART'S:** Hotel le Village St. Jean
- **MEXICO:** Even before the flu outbreak, "Good deals were plentiful along the Riviera Maya," says Nash. Her picks:
    Cancun: The Ritz Carlton, Le Méridien Cancun Resort & Spa, The Royal
    Playa del Carmen: Ceiba del Mar

* **Consider Puerto Rico.** Often a favorite destination for a short vacation or long-weekend getaway, particularly for those living along the East Coast in the U.S. But the island has numerous properties, many offering attractive off-season deals for a variety of wedding and honeymoon budgets. (And you don't need your passport, as you now do for other Caribbean locales.) Marta Albanese at the Puerto Rico Tourism Company gives us the scoop on her island.

  * RIO MAR BEACH RESORT & SPA has one of the most beautiful beaches on the eastern side of the island and the sunsets are spectacular. *wyndhamriomar.com*
  * EL CONVENTO HOTEL A luxury boutique hotel in the middle of Old San Juan. A little on the higher end but worth every penny. Very Old World charm with modern amenities and a great historic location. My sister was married at the cathedral across the street, held her reception at the hotel, and it was perfect. *www.elconvento.com*
  * EL CONQUISTADOR Located at the easternmost end of Puerto Rico and at the top of a cliff with amazing views to the sea and toward the small cays, Vieques and Culebra islands. They have their own private island for guests. *elconresort.com*
  * INN ON THE BLUE HORIZON A boutique property on Vieques Island, known for its beautiful beaches and laid-back island life. *innonthebluehorizon.com*
  * COPAMARINA BEACH RESORT Copamarina is a secluded resort, far from the glitz and nightlife of San Juan. I've seen sunset weddings at this property and they are beautiful. *www.copamarina.com*
  * CLUB SEABOURNE Great for a small, tropical wedding or honeymoon, on the very secluded island of Culebra. *www.clubseabourne.com*
  * ALSO CHECK OUT FOR VARIOUS PACKAGES: Conrad Condado Plaza (*condadoplaza.com*) and Hilton Ponce Golf & Casino Resort (*hiltoncaribbean. com*). For design buffs, the Normandie Hotel, an Historic National Landmark, known for its Art Deco architecture (*normandiepr.com*).

* **Over the pond:** *Can we afford Europe?* With the dollar strengthening against its all-time lows against the euro, is it time to consider a European honeymoon? Use mileage points to get you there and then consider some of the smaller, independent hotels, outside of Europe's most popular cities, particularly if you're traveling during peak summer months. And the deals are great off season. For example, in France: The Château de Saint Paterne (*chateau-saintpaterne.com*), a restored 15th-century chateau in Normandy recently featured in *Vogue*, has a pool, spacious parkland and doubles beginning at 135 euros. L'Hôtel Particulier in Arles (*hotel-particulier.com*), in Provence, a favorite of the French showbiz crowd, has doubles starting at 209 euros. In Italy, in the town of Laglio on Lago di Como near George Clooney's villa, there's Relais Regina Teodolinda (*relaisreginateodolinda.it*) with rates from 220 euros. Even the glamorous five-star Hotel Palácio Estoril (*palacioestorilhotel.com*) recently had discounts for double rooms for 150 euros during the month of June.

WEDDING PLANNER

Planning a wedding is a complicated, time-consuming affair requiring the organizational skill sets of a Broadway producer. If you're looking to maximize a wedding budget, you'll want (and need) extra time to research the best deals for everything from gowns to honeymoon locales.

9–12 months before

☐ Decide on the wedding's style: casual elegant, formal, informal.

☐ Consider where (traditional or alternative venue like a botanical garden or historical property) and when (month, day of week, time of day) you want the wedding to be held.

☐ Begin to look at ceremony and reception sites. If you're marrying in peak season, book them as soon as you decide. For outdoor locations, try to visit about the same time of year that your wedding will be held.

☐ Select an engagement ring.

☐ Rough out a budget, knowing who (family, or you and your fiancé) will pay for what.

☐ Draft the guest list.

☐ Determine how many attendants you'd like; you and your fiancé ask friends to be bridesmaids and groomsmen, parents of children who might serve as flower girls or ring bearers.

☐ Start bridal gown research. If you're buying vintage, the sooner you begin the process, the better.

☐ Set up your wedding website.

6–9 months before

☐ Finalize your choice of wedding gown and order. Reserve if you are renting.

☐ Once your gown is ordered, shop for accessories: veil or headpiece, shoes.

☐ Book ceremony and reception site if you haven't already.

☐ Choose the officiant for your ceremony and reserve his or her time.

☐ If you're not hiring a professional photographer, begin researching up-and-coming talent in photography and art programs at local colleges and universities.

☐ Set up bridal registry and/or travel registry. Link to your wedding site.

NOTES

4–6 months before

☐ Plan honeymoon and book travel arrangements (air, hotel, cruise), the earlier, the better if traveling in peak season.

☐ If you are working with a professional photographer, look at a variety of portfolios and reels. Hire photographer and videographer as soon as you make a decision.

☐ Select bridesmaids' and other attendants' dresses

☐ Will you be using a florist or doing the flowers yourself? When choosing a florist, research his or her work, discussing best-priced flowers in season for the month you'll marry. If you're organizing the flowers yourself, comparison shop among wholesalers online and locally. Estimate how extensive the time commitment will be to arrange flowers and whether you'll need to enlist friends and family.

☐ Figure out a system that will help you keep track of wedding gifts and thank-you notes. (Send out thank-yous as gifts arrive; avoids confusion and a daunting post-wedding task.)

3–5 months before

☐ Research and buy wedding rings.

☐ Are you having a cake? Interview bakers or caterers; test samples. If you're forgoing the cake, decide on other dessert options.

☐ Select stationery. If you're printing invitations yourself, research stationery kits and order card stock samples.

☐ Reserve or order the tuxedos or suits for the groom and his attendants.

☐ Finalize guest list.

☐ Will you be renting any special linens, chairs or lighting for the reception? If so, order as soon as you know your color scheme and number of guests.

☐ If you're going with live music at the ceremony, book the appropriate musical accompaniment.

☐ Decide on whether you'll hire a band or DJ for the reception and reserve.

☐ Research marriage license requirements for the place in which you'll marry. This is particularly important for destination weddings that take place outside the U.S.

☐ Make sure you and your fiancé have up-to-date passports, if you're traveling where they are required.

2 months before

☐ Send out invitations (generally six to eight weeks before the wedding; Save-the-Dates, obviously, can be sent out a month or two earlier).

☐ Provide travel information for out-of-town guests on your wedding website.

☐ Create ceremony and reception playlists if you're not working with a band or DJ.

1 month before

☐ Decide on transportation to and from ceremony and reception sites. Book limousine or other rental cars; research whether a vintage car might be an option. (Reserve transportation earlier if marrying in peak season.)

☐ Reserve the restaurant or venue for rehearsal dinner.

☐ Plan for final fitting (if required) for your wedding dress. Will one of your attendants need to help you with your gown? If so, schedule a practice session with the dress.

☐ Check if all documentation is in place for destination wedding outside U.S.

☐ Obtain the marriage license.

2 weeks before

☐ For the DIY-er, connect with all the friends and family members who volunteered to help with your decorations, flowers, etc. Make sure they're all still willing and able.

☐ Create shoot list for photographer, so no key family member or situation is overlooked.

☐ Select go-to person or persons (maid of honor, best man) for the day of the wedding to troubleshoot any problems that may arise, or answer any questions from caterers, musicians, photographers, etc.

☐ Create ceremony and reception seating plan.

☐ Follow up with anyone who hasn't RSVP'd. Give caterer or reception venue final guest count.

1 week before

☐ Dive into the details: Recheck everything—delivery and start times, addresses, contact people—with your vendors: florists, caterers, photographers, musicians, clothing rental companies, etc. Reconfirm all travel arrangements.

2 days before

☐ For the DIY bride, gather wedding volunteers to create decorations.

☐ Pack for your honeymoon travels; assemble all required documents.

1 day before

☐ Create floral arrangements if you and your friends are doing them.

☐ Oversee the set-up of reception decorations if you are doing them yourself and can access the venue.

☐ Have the mani-pedi after any DIY projects are finished.

☐ Reconfirm all details with the limo or car rental company: pickup times, locations, contact information.

☐ Go to rehearsal at the ceremony site, finalizing plans with the officiant, musicians, wedding party members. Determine order for the processional and recessional.

☐ Have a good time at the rehearsal dinner.

The day of the wedding

☐ Take a luxurious bath if you can spare the time; eat a good breakfast, or don't skimp on lunch if you're marrying later in the day. Allow yourself to be pampered if you're having hair and makeup done.

☐ Pat yourself on the back: You've survived all the preparations—congratulations! Slip into that gorgeous wedding dress and savor every moment of your ceremony and reception. Best wishes for a wonderful day!

NOTES

Resources

CHAPTER 1

celebritybrideguide.com:
For the latest on celebrity weddings

Marcy Blum, event planner and entertaining expert; marcyblum.com

CHAPTER 2

Ashley Garmon ashleygarmonphoto.com
Thomas Hager Photography
thomashagerphotography.com
Robert C. Mirani Photography
rcmphotography.com
Meg Perotti megperotti.com/blog
Our Labor of Love Photography
ourlaboroflove.com
ourblogoflove.com

CHAPTER 3

Get a copy of the FTC's "Wedding Gown Labels:
Unveiling the Requirements" at ftc.gov.

ONLINE VINTAGE STORES

antiquedress.com
cherishedbride.com
poshgirlvintage.com
vintagevixen.com
vintagewedding.com
Vintage patterns: sovintagepatterns.com and
    voguepatterns.com
Restoration and alteration: **thethreadbender.com,**
    contact Diana Ackerman
Cleaning and preservation: **heritagegown.com**

CONSIGNMENT SHOPS

Bridal Sense, 6600 Roswell Rd., Atlanta, GA
30328. T: 404-256-4696.
I Do Designer Bridal Consignment,
6742 West Belmont Ave., Chicago, IL 60634.
T: 773-205-1234.
Anonymously Yours, 9310 Forest Lane, Suite 204,
Dallas, TX 75243. T: 214-341-4618.
Michael's Bridal Salon, 1041 Madison Ave.,
New York, NY 10075. T: 212-737-7273.
I Do I Do Wedding Gowns, Gaither Center,
15932 Luanne Drive, Gaithersburg, MD 20877.
T: 240-243-0050.

E-BOUTIQUES

bravobride.com
encorebridal.com
oncewed.com
preownedweddingdresses.com
savethedress.com
woreitonce.com

RENTALS

alexandriasformal.com
llrental.com
onenightaffair.com

SAMPLE SALES

davidsbridal.com (Online sample sales only.)
Demetrios: 222 West 37th St., New York, NY
    10018. T: 212-967-5222.
Filene's Running of the Brides: filenesbasement.com
Hitchedsalon.com
Kleinfeld: 110 West 20th St., New York, NY, 10011.
    T: 646- 633-4300.
Monique Lhuillier: Call main store for info:
    323-655-1088.
saksfifthavenue.com
verawangonweddings.com

BRIDAL DISCOUNTERS

bridalonlinestore.com
bridecouture.com
bridepower.com
ebridalsuperstore.com
gownbidder.com
netbride.com.
perfectbridal.com
rkbridal.com
shopforbridal.com

STORES

Glamour Closet, 114 Columbus Ave., San
Francisco, CA 94133. T: 415-391-1515 and
324 S. La Brea Ave., Los Angeles, CA 90036.
T: 323-938-2000.
Neiman Marcus Last Call: nmlastcallstore.com

SHOWROOMS

The Bridal Building, 1385 Broadway, New York,
NY 10018. T: 212-764-5769.

NON-BRIDAL RETAILERS

anntaylor.com
bananarepublic.com
jcrew.com
spiegel.com

HEADPIECES AND VEILS

everafterbridalveils.com
illusionsbridal.com
save-on-crafts.com
veilshop.com
visionveils.com
weddingveil.com

BRIDAL FABRIC

bridalfabric.com
housefabric.com

FOR THE GROOM

jcrew.com
menswearhouse.com

CHAPTER 4

For information about purchasing diamonds:
Gemological Institute of America, gia.edu
For ring and stone price comparison, and general
information about diamonds: **pricescope.com**

VINTAGE RINGS

antiquejewelrymall.com

artdecodiamonds.com

ONLINE SOURCES

affordableweddingbands.com
bluenile.com
e-weddingbands.com
overstock.com
whiteflash.com

CULTURED STONES

apollodiamond.com
gemesis.com

MOISSANITE

moissanite.com

MAN-MADE STONES

diamondnexuslabs.com

CHAPTER 5

STATIONERS

elumdesigns.com
hautepapier.com
reavesengraving.com

WEDDING E-VITES

evite.com
paperlesspost.com

ONLINE STATIONERS

earthinvitations.com
ed-it.com
einvite.com
envelopperinc.com
finestationery.com
invitationhotline.com
reavesengraving.com
rexcraft.com

STATIONERY SUPPLIES

123print.com
dickblick.com
envelopperinc.com
lcipaper.com
mygatsby.com
paper-source.com

DESIGN TEMPLATES

123print.com
do-it-yourself-invitations.com
uniquityinvitations.com

WEDDING MAPS

weddingmapper.com

WEDDING WEBSITES

ewedding.com (free)
momentville.com (free)
mywedding.com (free)
weddingorg.com (fee-based)
weddingwindow.com (fee-based)
weddingwire.com (free)
wedpagedesigns.com (fee-based)
wedshare.com (fee-based)
wedsimple.com (fee-based)

oncewed.com
stylemepretty.com
wedding-photographers-directory.com

COMPREHENSIVE SITES
brides.com
theknot.com

COST COMPARISONS
costhelper.com
costofwedding.com

VENDOR RESEARCH
projectwedding.com
weddingwire.com
bbb.org Better Business Bureau

ACKNOWLEDGMENTS

It was a delight to be a part of so many weddings—if only vicariously—as this book was researched. A most sincere thanks to the couples who shared the stories of their weddings with us: Alyson Fox and Derek Dollahite; Virginia Miller and Patrick Barry; Ashley Summerlin and Dusty Meaders; Kristin LaMarre and Trent Snyder; Christa Scott and Travis Goldstein.

I'm also grateful to wedding and event planners extraordinare Leana Gallagher of The Events and Occasions Company, and Beth Helmstetter of Beth Helmstetter Events, for sharing their insights about wedding planning and for putting us in touch with stylish brides around the country, in Leana's case, Virginia Miller and Kristin LaMarre; with Beth, Christa Scott. And thanks, too, to Beth Newman of the wonderful website and blog *OnceWed.com*, for recommendations that lead us to Ashley Meaders and Alyson Fox.

It was a pleasure to speak with Lori Stephenson, owner of Lola Event Productions for a take on weddings, Chicago style, and Sarah Doheny of Sarah's Events & Bridal and Julia Erlichman of Julia & Friends Event Management about the events they have planned. Super talents Chris O'Dowd of The Cantering Cater and Mary Cleaver of the Cleaver Company shared many fresh and innovative ideas for wedding menus.

Any bride considering vintage should be as lucky as I was to chat at length with Jennifer Hollon of *CherishedBride.com* and Diana Ackerman of *TheThreadbender.com*. Their knowledge of other-era fashion and sewing techniques is extraordinary. Julie Jones of *EncoreBridal.com* and Laura Fluhr of New York City's Michael's were wonderfully helpful in explaining trends in the bridal gown market.

Billy Pry of BBJ Linen and Jan Cancila of The Linen House provided wonderful reception decorating ideas, and Brian Winthrop of Big Wave Productions and Brian King of BK the DJ, advice on lighting.

For our chapter on flowers, Mark Hayes of *Flowerbud. com* was an incredibly rich resource, and Sandra Pineda of *WholeBlossoms.com*, much appreciation for your creative thoughts. A very special nod to the incredibly talented Emily Candee of New York's Vine Floral & Event Design for her ideas and suggestions.

Thanks to Sarah Meyer Walsh and Erin Miller of Haute Papier for sharing their savvy about modern taste in wedding invitations. We were also able to glimpse the enormous creativity defining the contemporary wedding stationery market thanks to the innovative team at Paperless Post, and the pros at *MyGatsby.com* and *Envelopper.com*.

There were so many gifted photographers involved in this project—it was a pleasure to view your work: Meg Perotti, Thomas Hager, Ashley Garmon, Jesse Chamberlin at Our Labor of Love, Robert Mirani, Connie Miller of Studio Atticus, Tracey Brown, Rachel Robertson, Laura Moss, Laurie Rhodes, Leah Powell, and David Tucker. Our appreciation, too, to Chris Mann of *TropicalImaging.com* for his terrific advice on destination wedding photography.

Honeymoon travel pros Liliane Nash of the Humbert Travel Agency, Peggy Knipp of Honeymoons Galore, and Bambi Duvall of All About Travel shared their wise advice on stretching travel dollars, and their enticing descriptions of many tropical resorts could make anyone want to hop on the next plane, honeymoon or not. It was fascinating to speak with very knowledgable Jen Carfagno of The Weather Channel about weather in the tropics—her advice is essential for anyone heading south.

For those interested in celebrity bridal trends, don't miss Amy Sultan's *CelebrityBrideGuide.com*. A special thanks to her for the overview of this very rarefied slice of the weddings market. Marcy Blum, a celebrity and event planning pro, our appreciation for your insights, too.

And hats off to the stylish stylists whose work graces our pages: Courtney Keefe de Jauregui at Flush Designs and Chelsea Fuss, whose work we first saw on *OnceWed. com*, and Dan Pasky for his exquisite cake designs.

To Sharon Kenney at the Lyman Estate, and Nicole Griffin at the Seattle Art Museum, our thanks for tracking down images for their wonderful properties. A thanks, too, to the staff of *Save-on-crafts.com*, and Marta Albanese at the Puerto Rico Tourism Company.

The team at Filipacchi Publishing for their dedication and creativity: Patrice Fabricant for her wonderful design; Lauren Kuczala for her careful editing and the production team Lynn Scaglione and Annie Andres—much appreciation.

And my very special gratitude to Dorothée Walliser, Filipacchi Publishing's vice president/publisher, for her tireless work on every aspect of this project and for her great ideas, dedication, and for being such a pro to collaborate with.

PHOTO CREDITS

Page 1: Laura Moss; 2: Thomas Hager; 3: Rachel Robertson; 4: Thomas Hager; 5: Rachel Robertson (both); 6: Rachel Robertson; 9: Leah Powell; 10: Rachel Robertson (both); 11: Thomas Hager; 12–17: Ashley Garmon; 18–21: Robert Mirani; 22–25: Our Labor of Love; 26–29: Meg Perotti; 30–34: Thomas Hager; 36: Studio Atticus; 37: Thomas Hager; 38: Ashley Garmon; 39: Courtesy of Posh Girl Vintage; 40: Our Labor of Love; 42: Thomas Hager; 43, 44: Studio Atticus; 45, 46, 47: Laura Moss; 48, 49: Ashley Garmon; 50: Laura Moss; 51, left: Laura Moss; 51, right: Studio Atticus; 52: Ashley Garmon; 54: Courtesy of Antique Jewelry Mall; 55: Courtesy of Apollo Diamonds; 56, top: Meg Perotti; 56, bottom: Laura Moss; 57: Meg Perotti; 58: Our Labor of Love; 60, top: Courtesy of Paperless Post; 60, bottom: Our Labor of Love; 61, from top to bottom: Elum, Elum, Haute Papier; 63: Courtesy of Envelopper Inc.; 64, 65, 66: Courtesy of *MyGatsby.com*; 67: Courtesy of Envelopper Inc.; 70: Rachel Robertson; 73: Courtesy of Copamarina Beach Resort & Spa; 74: Kate Sears; 75, left: Laurie Rhodes; 75, right: Mary Ellen Bartley; 76: Meg Perotti (both); 77, left: Courtesy BBJ Linen/Lily Mayfield; 77, right: Meg Perotti; 78, top: Jacqueline Hopkins; 78, bottom: Charles Schiller; 79: Courtesy of Seattle Olympic Sculpture Park/Clare Marie Photography; 80: Karyn Millet; 81, top left and bottom right: Courtesy of The Ribault Club/Leah Powell; 81, top right: Courtesy of The Ribault Club; 82: Sang An; 83: Rachel Robertson; 84, left: Charles Schiller; 84, center top and bottom: Laurie Rhodes; 85: Laura Moss; 86: Courtesy BBJ Linen/Clay Jackson Photography; 87: Courtesy of Seattle Asian Art Museum/Justin Gollmer; 88, 89: Courtney Keefe de Jauregui/Flush Designs; 90: Meg Perotti; 91: Dan Pasky/*dandanbakingco.com*; 92: Thomas Hager; 93: Laura Moss (both); 95: Laurie Rhodes; 96: Courtesy of Seattle Art Museum/John and Joseph Photography; 98: David Tucker; 100: Courtesy of Historic New England; 101, top: Courtesy of Seattle Olympic Sculpture Park/Clare Marie Photography; 101, bottom: Courtesy of Seattle Art Museum/John and Joseph Photography; 102: Courtesy of Miami Beach Botanical Garden; 103, left: Courtesy of The Commandant's House/Brian Phillips Photography; 103, right: Courtesy of Municipal Building Commission/Minneapolis City Hall and Hennepin Courthouse/Tracey Snead; 104: Courtesy of The Bridges Golf Club/Jay Solomon Photography; 105, left: Studio Atticus; 105, right: Laura Moss; 106: Thomas Hager; 107: Ashley Garmon; 108: Leah Powell; 110, 111: Laura Moss; 112: Meg Perotti; 113: Courtesy of Vine Floral & Event Design/Emily Candee; 114: Chelsea Fuss; 115, left: Thomas Hager; 115, right: Ashley Garmon; 116: Courtesy of Seattle Olympic Sculpture Park/Clare Marie Photography; 117: Laura Moss (both); 118: Ashley Garmon; 119, top left: Laurie Rhodes; 119, top right: Thomas Hager; 119, bottom: Meg Perotti; 120: Laurie Rhodes; 122: Laura Moss; 123: Leah Powell; 124: Laurie Rhodes; 126: Courtesy of The Antigua & Barbuda Tourist Office/Geoff Howes; 128: Courtesy of The Cayman Islands Department of Tourism/Dave Taylor; 130: Courtesy of U.S. Virgin Islands Department of Tourism; 132: Courtesy of The Jamaica Tourist Board; 135: Courtesy of The Antigua & Barbuda Tourist Office/Geoff Howes; 136: Courtesy of The Puerto Rico Tourism Company/El San Juan Hotel & Casino.